OUR STORY

Della Toadlena

Order this book online at www.trafford.com
or email orders@trafford.com

Most Trafford titles are also available at major online book retailers.

Printed in the United States of America.

ISBN: 978-1-4269-3461-2 (sc)
ISBN: 978-1-4269-3462-9 (e-book)

*Our mission is to efficiently provide the world's finest, most comprehensive book publishing
service, enabling every author to experience success. To find out how to publish your book,
your way, and have it available worldwide, visit us online at www.trafford.com*

Trafford rev. 08/04/2010

 www.trafford.com

North America & international
toll-free: 1 888 232 4444 (USA & Canada)
phone: 250 383 6864 ♦ fax: 812 355 4082

ACKNOWLEDGEMENTS

I wish to thank certain individuals without whom this book will not have been possible. My granddaughter, Steph, helped me stay focused on the details of my computer, and my nephew, Garrick, offered technical support. My children, Brent and Leigh Ann, put the images on the cover and the interior of the book together, and Nelaine Shorty, was instrumental in carrying out the e-proofing on the proofing guide.

NIHAHANE'

My dear children and grandchildren:

I write this story for you, so you will know where we came from as Naashgali Dine'e, and where we have been. I cannot tell you where you will go, for that belongs to the future, but I hope that from this story you will glean the direction I hope you will go. Even today in 2008, some of you don't know the story of our origin. It is very simple, and I will tell it to you now. Then I will proceed to tell you the autobiographical account of what I remember as I was growing up.

Our roots begin with Mescalero Woman, an Apache captive brought back by a group of Navajo warriors from a raiding expedition. This event had to have happened before the infamous Long Walk, for Navajos were forbidden to go raiding after that. Story says that after a long winter, young warriors from Black Rock, Tsaile, and Wheatfields area were restless from all the inactivity of winter. Early that spring, a bunch of them left on horseback to raid ranches of Mexicans, Whites, and Pueblos down south.

When the raiders returned in midsummer, the people were living in Shash Bitoo or Bear Spring a small area in Black Rock. Bears were said to have come down from the mountain to drink at the spring. Along with horses, cattle, mules, and sheep, they brought an Apache woman. Sources say she sat astride a horse with her hands tied behind her. She was covered with dust from head to toe, and her hair was bushy and tangled with debris. She was dragged kicking and screaming to the base of the mountain that rose above camp and tied to a dead pinon stump. Dry tree stumps

1

were maintained in the old days to preserve fire. Someone was delegated to keep coals alive through the day to prevent the fire from going out.

There she remained for many days, being untied only to be fed or so she could relieve herself. Once she tried an attempt at escape with a knife she had concealed from an earlier feeding. When the man untied here to let her eat, she flung herself on the poor, unsuspecting individual, waving the knife in the air. Others heard the commotion, though, and came running to subdue her, and that was the last time she tried to escape.

Eventually, I supposed she resigned herself to the fact that she would never return to her homeland and family and began to accept the ways of her captors. With the coming of fall she was untied and allowed to go about camp, helping the women with various chores of camp life. She was also allowed to go into the hogan of one of the families to sleep at night. Someone must have thrown a wrap of some kind across the hearth for her to cover herself with from the late, cold autumn nights.

Later she is said to have married one of her captors. And because she had no clan, a Navajo clan was created for her and her future offspring. This came to be the adopted clan called Naasgali Dine'e. This great, great, great grandmother of ours came to be known as Naasgali Azdzaan.

As a child I remember sitting up late at night with my sisters helping Grandma, Asdzaan Altsisi and our mother preparing food for the next day. Often it was roasting and grinding corn into meal for cornbread, pudding, dumpling or mush. Asdzaan Altsisi was our mother's paternal grandmother. My mother was just three when her mother died, and this old lady took her under her wings and raised her. She was already a very old woman with white hair when we lived with her. Another time when there had been the butchering of a sheep, it was peeling the inside lining of the skin and running skewers of fat through it.

That was my favorite time when grandmother told us stories. Every night we crowded around her to hear stories of long ago. Grandmother Asdzaan Alts'isi always said she was four years old when she returned with the people from (Hweeldi) Fort Sumner. She said this was true because she could climb onto the side step of a wagon, emphasizing a three year old could not do that. If this is the case, she was seventy-seven years old when I was born, and in her 80's later when we lived with her. Her family said she lived to be past one hundred when she died of old age. I remember a sprite, very active woman. She was soft spoken, too, never raising her voice harshly even when my sisters and I must have been naughty. She was busy from dawn until late at night preparing corn food for the days to come.

Even mother listened intently as she spun and carded wool for a rug she was working on although she must have heard the story a hundred times. Our only light came from the fire burning inside the sawed-off barrel stove. Sometimes we had a kerosene lamp, but most of the time Grandma's rambunctious grandsons knocked against it in their wrestling and broke it. Sometimes she burned out the bottom of a glass jar and fashioned a would-be chimney for the lamp. It worked. When we were snowed in from the outside world, we improvised and lived the best we could.

There are no documents of dates available to account for these activities, only what Grandmother Alts'sisi and her daughter, Standing Rock Woman, told to us. (In a workshop on Oral History, long after I was working, I heard that word of mouth was just as valid as written history). As we grew older, a maternal uncle, Joe Begay, who had been to the Korean Conflict also used to relate the story to us as we sat under the brush arbor in summer during one of his visits. As with all stories, this one was carried on by word of mouth as I'm doing here but through word processing.

It is also unclear how many generations have passed since the bringing of Mescalero Woman. The story always started as "Alk'idaa' jini, t'ah anaa' daholoodaa'" (A long time ago when people were still warring with enemies). Your sister or Aunt Tanya Johnson took on this woman's name. Before she married, around about her first menses or Kinaalda, her mother Evelyn patted her all over saying that from here on she will take on the name of her ancestor and be called Naashgali Asdzaan. This was one of the ways people were given names in the old days.

When Mescalero Woman was going to marry one of the men that captured her, a meeting was held to determine a clan for her and her future offspring. Because all Navajo clans have other clans they are related to, new people coming into the tribe also had to have clans related to them. Navajos were always very receptive to people of other tribes coming in and created clans for them. At the meeting, a Deeshchiinii person said, "My clan will be related to this new group." In this way we are related to this clan and all the clans that are related to them. I understand they include, Tsi'naajinii, Kinlichiinii, and Tl'aashchi'i.

It is unknown how many children came from this union. We have asked some elders, but none of them remembered. The problem is that we began inquiring too late after the people from that generation had gone on. Today there are families in Chinle and Many Farms, Arizona with grandparents who are Naashgali Dine'e, and they say these grandparents once said they came from Black Rock where a Mescalero woman was supposed to have been brought. For some reason, mom, Asdzaan Alts'isi, her daughter, and Uncle Joe did not think it was important to speak of them.Maybe these grandparents are the descendants of that first pair.

Growing up, we were always told to ask someone we are interested in what his/her clan is, for the consequences of clan incest are not very pretty. "It breeds illness, poverty, and death," we were told. I know many young people do not think clan relationships are important anymore, that they were meant for the old days. When I was teaching writing at Dine College, I heard them say and write that they hate the Navajo clan system and wished there were no clans. "Every time I meet a new guy, he is related to me," cried one young lady, one day.

Once I asked a Blessing Way practitioner if the old teachings indeed no longer worked and that they were meant for an older time. He sat thinking for a moment and then asked, "Does the sun still come up? Do the seasons still come and go? Is there still births and old age of people? And does the fire still burn"? I replied "yes." Then these things are as true today as they were at the beginning of time," he admonished me as if I was the one disbelieving.

"You are not Navajo," Grandma would say on those long winter nights. "Your grandmother was an Apache captive (yisnaah)." Then she would proceed to relate to us what she remembered of the story told to her. She even said in the future people might make fun of us because of our clan. Ironically, it was one of her granddaughters who later taunted me and my sisters. She used to dance up and down, clapping her hands saying, "Ha, Ha! You are not Navajos; you have no relatives," very much like you would say when you have to kill a spider, "Nik'ei adin," until she brought me to tears. It bothered me more than my sisters who just ran off when she got started. I yelled for her to stop. "Don't say that; you are a liar!" I sobbed.

Outside, snow would be falling softly on the dirt roof of our hogan. What came down the smoke-hole sizzled on the stove top. Soon everyone fell asleep, snuggled warmly in their sheepskin bedding. Shadows of firelight through the holes in the stove danced and made strange images on the walls and ceiling. I lay awake for awhile listening to the soft breathing of the others, picturing a terrified woman running from a bunch of men on horseback.

Ever since then and even today, I wonder what she must have felt on that long journey to Navajo land. I also wonder if she left any children behind, for she was to have been of childbearing age. Did she have a husband, parents, brothers, sisters, and grandparents that she left behind?

We'll never know. As I expressed earlier, many stories similar to ours abound. People will come up to you and say they are descendants of Mescalero Apache, too, not necessarily our Mescalero Woman, but that is their story. Each story will be slightly different, but the underlying theme will always be that of abduction. Just remember this story that I tell to you, though, from my memory of what Asdzaan Alts'isi told to my sisters and me on those long winter nights.

Not much more was said about Naasgali Asdzaan or her descendants until I was ready to go to school. At that point, I guess to put me at ease about going away to school, mother revealed to me that her mother had also gone to school with a sister. It is not clear where they went to school, though. Some people said it was at the Saint Micheals Catholic Mission School in St. Micheals, Arizona while others said it was at the Fort Defiance Boarding School.

One summer day, the girls returned home to Bear Spring. That same day a man from Many Farms, Arizona came on horseback and whisked one of the girls away to be his wife. The other one stayed behind and later married a local man named Hastiishtelini,biye'(Son of the Late Wide Man). She was our grandmother, mine and yours. We also know there were one other sister and a brother; however, there may have been more. Our grandmother and her new husband stayed on the land where Mescalero Woman was brought and raised their children.

Mother's grandfather (Niltahini') developed this land in Black Rock or more specifically, Bear Spring, while the children were growing up and some of them were going to school. He put a fence of logs around a field where he grew corn and squash. I remember seeing this log fence before it deteriorated into the ground. My grandparents had four men and two women with my mother being the youngest. Mother said her father's people told her that her mother died of (atsa'as a), something like a tumor or growth in the stomach. Black Rock, as you know, is a tiny community with only a handful of people living there.

Niltahini' was mother's maternal grandfather. This makes me think that his wife's mother was Mescalero Woman, the captive. The story says he was a short and slight man. Once, he and some men were out hunting when he became separated from them. As he was walking, trying to find his party, he saw a bunch of horsebacks riding fast toward him. With no time to run for cover, he threw himself down on the ground and lay flat on his front, as even as he could, with the road. The enemy did not see him and just rode over him. It's a wonder he was not trampled by the horses.

That's how his party found him, lying flat or even with the land, and thus his name: Lying Flat or Even with the Land.

There is a place in Canyon Del Muerto, past Standing Rock at the entrance to the Many Juniper Berry Trail, (Tsidzelani) where two reddish marks appear high above the rock wall. Story says that Lying Flat and another man came here and put their marks on the rock wall with red paint (chiih) so they could be remembered for all time. When you look up at the marks, there is no possible way an individual could have gotten up there. Mother used to say that back then people had special powers that allowed them to carry out unexplainable feats. You young disbelieving guys used to say, "No Way! There's no way anyone could have climbed up there and down into the overhang!" I'm reminded of James Welche's protagonist who communicates with Raven in *Fools Crow* which is a novel set in the 1700's when stuff like this were still possible in Native American life.

Years later, the family of the lady that used to make me cry tried to claim ownership of the small plot of land that mother raised ten children on in Bear Spring. She stood steadfast with all her might against this strong Navajo family made up of medicine people, refusing to let her guard down. As we were growing up, she instilled in us the importance of land and how without it we are nothing. She singled out your Uncle Benjamin and made sure he understood the exact boundary of the land we were to protect from others who would try to claim it.

See, people, especially mother's paternal group thought since we are of Apache descent, they could take advantage of us, but they did now know how our mother was once she had her mind set on something. Annie Tully Begay or Altsxohaasbaa' was a very outspoken woman. Like her great grandmother who was dragged fighting all the way to the pinon stump before her, mother adamantly protected what she knew rightfully belonged to her. Of course you know she was not formally educated.

Because mother was raised by her paternal grandmother, she was expected to be part of that family. By the way, this family is of the Coyote Pass or Ma'iideeshgiizhii Clan. She moved around with them to summer and winter camps. When she began to have children and her family began to grow, she must have become concerned about a home base to raise them on. The land she and her paternal family moved to for summer forage was Bear Spring, where Mescalero Woman was first brought. However, they began to settle on it. Their rationale must have been that they raised her, so they had every right to do so.

This Coyote Pass family had/has a large, beautiful summer camp in Canyon Delmuerto and a winter camp at Middle Point on top of the south rim of this canyon. Mother tried to get them to move, but by the time I was twenty-two and married to Chei Lee, the family had started to build within the boundary mother had arbitrarily drawn up. Of course Grandma Asdzaan Alts'si had long ago died of old age.

From what I can remember, mother's arbitrary boundary begins on the northeast where the main road from Tsaile comes across an old cornfield called Haskelbahi Bi Da'ak'eh or Gray Boy's Cornfield. It is overgrown with thick sagebrush today with no indication there was ever a cornfield. A small arroyo begins just before a little rise and runs all the way into a large wash below Blackwood Forest. This wash forms the eastern boundary. Then the wash runs southward for a couple of miles before it swings westward. That is the extent of the boundary marked by the big wash. It picks up again about a mile above the wash at a place called Tselgai si'ani. Here, it runs northward up the mountain all the way to Dark Cave or Tseyaachahalheel where one of our great grandmothers used to winter. From there it runs eastward and comes down to Gray Boy's Cornfield.

As mother discussed the land base, we wrote it down and gave it to our father for safe-keeping. Shortly after that mother set up an important meeting at her home and invited many tribal government officials, medicine people, and elders from the community. She butchered a fat two-year old lamb and prepared pots of stew and piles of fry bread. Following the mutton feast, she let people know why she had brought them together. Somehow she must have known she was not going to be much longer and she wanted to make them aware of what was rightfully hers and her children's, passed on to the Naashgali Dine'e Clan by her grandfather, Nilt'ahini'

She impressed upon those in attendance that her children were growing up and would need places to raise their own children. After presenting her case, she asked them to tell the Coyote Pass family to move off her land. The leaders listened intently to mother's request and found her points convincing. Respectfully, they asked the family to move that indeed they had two suitable homesteads as opposed to this woman's one. The family was not going to take this ruling quietly. They rebutted saying their grandmother, Little Woman's daughter, was an old woman. "Was Altsxohaasbaa' really going to throw an old woman away out into the cold?" Well, the leaders reconsidered and then decided, "When the old woman dies of old age, everyone else has to move away and leave this small land base to the tiny Naashgali family. These were the exact words of the old leaders. Reluctantly, our mother agreed.

Three years after this meeting, mother died. She fell down and never regained consciousness. Nothing was out of the ordinary on this typical spring day, but suddenly mom was dead. She and your Grandpa Harry had come to Chinle to check my younger brothers and sisters out from boarding school. After she and the kids came to pick me up at the Chinle Clinic where I worked, we returned to the Garcias Trading Post. Mom had forgotten to buy a jar of chili peppers the kids love to eat with mutton ribs she had bought earlier. She seldom checked them out, so this was a treat for them. Everyone stayed in the truck while mom and I walked toward the trading post. Half way to the entrance way, mom fell forward on her face. While some men there tried to give her mouth-to-mouth, someone called the clinic from where I had just left. Dr Singer, one of the clinic doctors, had not gone home yet, so he came with the ambulance. He tried to resuscitate her too but to no avail. He told us mom died of a massive stroke, and that she did not feel anything.

This is a day that we never forget. Mom used to comment on spring being the most beautiful season of the year when all things came to life. Once I heard her say, "It would be very sad indeed to die in the spring." Sometimes I wonder about the irony of her comment and of how and when she died. The day that began so perfectly, ended so tragically, leaving its ugly scar on my father, my siblings, and me forever. The summer before she left, she also took your Chei Lee and me aside and asked him to always look after her children and not let them wander. We were surprised at her action at the time, but today we know she already felt she did not have too long to live, and she wanted her children to be cared for.

The summer our mom died, your uncles, aunts, and I wanted to review the boundary she had set out and to let the younger children know of its existence. However, we could not find the notebook in which we had drawn the map that summer day. Our father said he had put it in an old metal suitcase where he kept important things. We were devastated, for without it we had no proof! Anyone of mother's paternal people could build any place they wanted. We made Benjamin think very hard to remember where mom had set the boundary.

And build they did, right inside the boundary, disregarding the words of the leaders three years before. Their grandmother had been gone for a couple of years now. Instead of moving away, they added to the crumbling square house a shade house and corrals for their animals. No amount of talking to them did any good. They just accused us of not being sympathetic and being disrespectful. By now, it was just my brothers, sisters, and me. Our father, a quiet man was there, but what he had to say was no good; he was only an in-law. This dispute was between the Naashgali Dine'e and Ma'iideeshgiizhnii Clans.

One day, this squatter family requested the electric company out of Chinle to run a line to their frame house. My brothers stopped the company from extending electricity to their home, for these guys were trying to make their stay on mom's homestead more than permanent. Usually, the family lived with its elder mother in a housing project in Chinle, year round. For this occasion, the family brought the mother to Black Rock just at the end of summer.They claimed the nights were too dark and too cold, and she needed lighting to get from the house to the outdoor privy and back. Oh, we went round and round, trying to talk some sense into these people, even reminding them what the elders had stipulated that long ago time, but it did no good. Eventually, though, they gave up and moved their mother back to their warm, lighted house in Chinle.

My siblings were young men and women now and had started families, and they started expanding mother's homestead. The boys built a large, red hay barn, a corral large enough to hold many cattle and horses, and a grain field to grow feed for the animals. Even your aunt Victoria built a small barn and a fence for her horses. My sisters Betty and Alice had houses built, your Chei Lee built a ceremonial hogan, and more recently Benjamin built a hogan. Thus, just as our mother and your grandmother had predicted, we were growing up and expanding, and there were still you children coming up. The intention was to make this family aware that we were serious about developing our departed mother's land and living on it that it was not just there for the taking. In the past they were known to have said that Altsxohaasbaa's children were not interested in the land, for they never come back to the land base anymore.

Thus, it is up to you young people, my sisters' and my children, to see that our family land base remains intact. Build on it, even if it is just a shade arbor. Your uncles Chet and Ben were always harping on that idea. Fight for the land; don't let others move on it under false pretenses.

Our father, Pa, later told us that one time an older brother of his who was married to the woman that used to make me cry by telling me I had no relatives, asked him to allow him a small space where he could settle his family down. "Just for the summer," I understand he said, "Until I can get a larger place from my in-laws." This was shortly after mother died, and

Pa let him settle on a small patch of land just inside the boundary mom had pointed out for us to protect close to Dark Cave. I don't know why Pa did this, but mother would never have stood for it. Now the children of that couple are grown and are calling this place their very own, how it was handed down to them by their parents.

MIGRATION

The earliest I remember of moving around with my mother's paternal family and living in Canyon DelMuerto at a place called Standing Rock is when I was three years old. I remember playing outside with the other children in camp. Shortly, I wanted to be with my mother, so I dashed inside the hogan to be with her. I have a blurred recollection of women sitting on both sides of the Hogan and my mother sitting in the center, hanging onto a rope suspended from the roof beams. An old woman sat behind her. I remember so well a hand reaching out of the crowd of women and jerking me back as I ran to my mother's side. My mother was giving birth to your Aunt Evy, and that was why all the women were there.

Standing Rock was the spring camp of my mother's paternal people. Though her father was remarried, he had allowed a few heads of sheep to remain with his people's herd for her after her mother died. To this place in the canyon this group moved every spring from their winter camp above the southern rim for the sheep to lamb, to sheer the thick winter wool from the sheep, and to plant seeds of corn, watermelon, cantaloupe, squash, and beans in the ground. There was also a large peach orchard to hoe weeds under and to water. Just behind the large, looming Standing Rock on the north side of camp was a small patch of field that my grandfather had passed on to his daughter. Two small peach trees stood on an incline from the rock where water ran down the tall rock to feed the fruit trees. Here, mom used to take us when the other people of camp were eating supper, and she didn't have any food to cook for us. We played on the rock while mother sat under the peach trees spinning wool.

After the last seed was put into the ground, mother would take my younger sister and me with her to stay a few days with her sister at a place called Kini or simply House, just before Twin Trails. This place got its name because it was the very first square house built in the canyon for people to live in. Of course the other square or rectangular houses were built by the Anasazi or Ancient Ones high up in the rock walls of the canyon.

My older sister who was eight or nine was left behind to look after the newly plowed field because squirrels scurried down from the rocky base of the canyon walls, dug up the seeds, and carried them off. If left unattended, we would have nothing to harvest in the fall and nothing to eat in the winter was mother's rationale. She had to keep up a noisy commotion to scare the critters away, which was not hard to do when all the children of camp came to join her. As I grew older, I got a chance to help her, but for some reason mother did not want me to do that chore all the time. That was fun, though, making all kinds of commotion and pretending to be white tourists. We pretended to talk English, looking through make-believe binoculars at high rock walls. We also banged on tin cans, sang at the top of our lungs, and we laughed and we cried hard when we got hurt.

At Kini lived my aunt, her husband, and their three children. He was also the father of us three girls. Sometimes as my mother was growing up, her sister would take her from Grandma Alts'isi's home to have her stay with her and her husband at Kini. I guess that is how we older sisters came to be. I have heard mother was just eleven, when she had my older sister. They lived on one of the best farming lands in the canyon that they irrigated before they planted, unlike the dry farming we practiced at Standing Rock. Their sheep they kept with his mother's herd at a place called Big Cave further up the canyon. Our father was even a medicine man, practicing the Chirichaua Way that took him away for days at a time. For Navajos, they were considered wealthy.

While mom helped her sister to spin and card wool, put up a loom to weave a rug, and catch up on news and gossip from the long winter, my cousin and I explored the surrounding area. Once we found some large, beautiful white flowers growing against the rock walls. We picked them and brought home an armful. Our mothers were so upset when they saw what we had done. They screamed at us to take them away and not ever bother them again. You see, we had brought home Datura or Jimson Weed that only a medicine man who knew its sacred name was supposed to handle. Soon it was time to return to Standing Rock to hoe weeds in the newly sprouted cornfield and to prepare to move to Black Rock, the summer camp. This was about late May.

Mother had married Pa, Kenneth Clark, at her father's insistence. I understand he said, "You can't just continue to have babies by your older sister's husband; find your own." Rather than allowing his daughter to find her own man, he went in search of a man that would be kind to his daughter and help her raise her girls. I don't know how he did it, but I like to think he found the right man for her. Pa was always away working on the railroad, but he and mother had seven children: four sons and three daughters.

My brothers gave our father the name, Pa. As children they loved watching western movies, with their father, "Bonanza" being their favorite. In the show, the men called their father Pa. Soon the name stuck, and he became Pa to everyone in the community.

Pa was a strong, hardworking man. A man of few words, he never complained as he helped mom raise ten children. Mother's stepmother used to compare him to a mule, always working in the cornfield, tinkering with this and that, and carrying heavy loads on his back. When mother had finished a rug or there were dried sheep or goat skins available, he'd saddle his horse and ride to Chinle to buy food at the Garcias or Thunderbird Trading Post. He rode his horse down the Mummy Cave Trail (Tseyaakini), down the canyon floor, up the northern Twin Trail (Alnaasha'atiin) to the Delmuerto community, and then twelve miles into Chinle. Sometimes he loaded food and other necessities on his horse and rode it back. Sometimes when the load was too heavy, he just led his horse all the way home, a good twenty-five miles. Most times, he'd come home in the middle of the night and mother would wake us up to eat tortillas she'd been saving from supper to dip in bacon fat from the slab bacon Pa brought from the store.

Sometimes there was an orange in the pack my father brought from the trading post. Mother would hold it back until the next day when she would peel it and separate it into sections. Then she gave each one of us a slice. I would hold it in my mouth savoring the sweet juice. That was all everyone got, one slice, but I used to wish for a whole peeled orange that I could sink my teeth into and eat all by myself.

Then mother would soak the orange peelings in a large cup of water and let it sit for a while. Later, she would have us take a sip of it and pass it until everyone got a sip. Those were the days when there was not enough food, but our mother made sure we got something although it meant she didn't get her share.

One of the families in the camp remained behind to look after the fields and orchards while the rest of us drove the sheep up the Many Juniper Berries Trail. Some of the elders led horses laden with belongings while others walked, carrying small children or other loads on their backs. Moving was such a happy occasion, anticipating new grass for the sheep and a change of scenery for us. Even the animals were excited: dogs ran to and fro, yipping; chickens squawked and fluttered their wings trying to escape their cages; horses pricked their ears; and sheep baaed and milled around, eager to get going. We older children went with the sheep, ahead of everyone. It was very slow going, with the sheep stopping to nibble on wild rose bushes or to lick salty rock lichen on the trail. Once on top, though, all chaos broke loose, for by now the yucca was in full bloom. The sheep scattered in search of these succulent flowers they had not tasted in a year. Eventually, everyone arrived at the summer camp.

About a month later, around the beginning of July, it got very hot at summer camp. The water holes dried, and the grass withered under the hot summer sun. Owl-feet brush grew wild on the prairie, and when the sheep ate too much of it, they became sick and vomited. Then mother decided it was time to drive the sheep back into the canyon, this time to her mother-in-law's summer camp at Charcoal Rock (Tsebik'ina'asht'eszhi). We usually cut our small herd from Asdzaa' Alts'isi's herd and drove them to the canyon. Charcoal Rock is a place beyond Mummy Cave, a few miles below the Tsaile Dam.

It was usually much cooler here than any other place in the canyon because it is close to the mountain. The stream never dried up and grass was always green and plentiful. Cloudbursts and flash floods were frequent here, and many times my sisters or brothers and I would be trapped on the other side of the wash with the sheep. This was a wonderful place to spend one's childhood although it was very remote. I heard years ago, people (some closely related to us) shut themselves off from the rest of the world in this canyon and engaged in activities that were not compatible with the teachings of our people. However, that is a whole different story all together. A short distance from our camp grew clusters of blueberry bushes where we spent our afternoons eating to our hearts' content. A large cottonwood tree grew by our camp, and millions of tiny, black ants lived at its base. When we stepped on them, they put forth an acrid stench. Much later in school I tasted blue cheese salad dressing for the first time, and it reminded me of that smell.

By now, the sheep would be nice and fat, and school would be about to start at the boarding school in Chinle. It would be August and some corn would be ripening along with sweet red plums. It was time to move out to Kits'iili, a summer camp that also belonged to Pa's family. Mom had been busy all summer long weaving rugs to sell at the trading post to buy school clothes. To supplement the income from the rugs, mother also sold fat lambs to people living in the canyon. People just loved the meat because for some reason, their sheep did not get as fat as mom's.

While we resided at Kits'iili, we made trips to Standing Rock to check on our corn field. Alas, it never produced very much. At the time, I did not understand why mom continued to have the field plowed and planted every spring. What the squirrels and rabbits did not devour, the long hot, dusty summer simply withered. Much later the two peach trees behind Standing Rock did yield a little.

During this time, also, we stopped off at my aunt's at Kini. Here the harvest was plentiful. Fat ears of corn grew on every cornstalk; the peach trees were laden with large, white and red peaches; huge green and yellow melons sat on vines; and the hay field was full of tall, fragrant alfalfa ready for cutting. During the day mom helped her sister char ears of corn, prepare and dry kneel-down-bread, and barbecue corn in a hot pit for the long winter. Once more my cousin and I explored, and sometimes our curiosity got the best of us. Though there were melons galore to be had in his parents' field, we found very exciting stealing Atsiddy's melons. One time we cut small holes in every melon to see which ones were red. Taking all the red ones, we stashed them in some weeds in the wash, and of course, they all turned bad before we could eat all of them. We were just the worst kids, for all Atsiddy's melon crop was ruined that year. When he came to inquire if we know anything of the incident, we made matters worse by lying and blaming someone else, saying he was carrying a knife the other day. In the evening, we returned to Kits'iili

GOING TO
BOARDING SCHOOL

I remember leaving my mother's Hogan at age five going on six, to go to boarding school for the first time. There was a mixed feeling of excitement over starting something different and sadness because I was going to leave home for the first time. I was just a child by some people standards, but in another way I was already mom's big helper around the home. By this time I knew how to build a fire, put on a pot of water to dye wool, card wool, and sit by mom and help her make yarn. Sometimes, she let me put in a line or two of yarn into the rug she was working on. I was also old enough to take the sheep out alone.

Early that autumn morning, I scrambled out of my sheepskin bedding and headed outside. Mom was busy flapping dough back and forth between her hands for fry bread while a pot of mutton and fresh corn stew bubbled and boiled on some ashes scattered out of the sawed-off barrel that was our stove.

Outside, the sun had come over the eastern rim of Canyon Del Muerto and shining brightly. My father Pa stood by the wagon repairing something on the harness while the two horses ate heartily of the fresh corn cobs he had chopped up for them. Quickly, I ran to my little play area to say good-bye to the tiny figures of people and animals I had constructed out of clay. I rearranged them far back in the tiny caves of the rock wall above the peach orchard where they probably remain today, untouched by wind or rain.

As I dashed back into the hogan I saw that mom was just beside herself over something. Some of her father's people who lived in that camp and my father were there, discussing something I did not understand. After much confusion, I learned mom was all flustered over the fact that I did not have an English name. None of the people gathered had been to school either, so they had no ideas about names. Of course there was my childhood name, but mom thought it would be absurd to show up at the school and say, "This is Asdzaa Yazhi, or Little Woman." I, however, could not understand how that would be absurd. It was my name!

Just at that time, Uncle Joe Begay, the veteran, happened by and saved the day. When the problem was presented to him, he thought for a while and said, "Call her Della!" Thus, I have been Della ever since.

After that problem was resolved, mom, dad, two women from the camp and I were piled in the wagon on our way out of the canyon. Dad whistled a tune, mom and the women were deep in conversation about something, while I sat and thought about what going to school and being away from home were going to be like. I pressed very close to mother as if to draw enough of her into me to last all the time I was going to be away. We drove the wagon up to the old Garcia Trading Post, and dad unhitched the horses. He let them drink water from a common watering hole where everyone coming from the outlying areas watered their horses.

Garcias was one of the first trading posts in the area, but I know none of you is old enough to remember that. It was run by a Mexican family out of Albuquerque, NM. Today the Holiday Inn motel and restaurant sit right there. At the store, mom bought a set of new clothes for me. I remember a pair of pastel yellow socks. In addition to the one set of new clothes, there was a flour sack of used clothing and shoes she got from the Presbyterian Church. Today, I am appalled at how kids refuse to wear anything except $100.00 brand name shoes, and parents buy them for their children even though they may not be able to afford them. Kids refuse to wear shoes from Wal-Mart or Pay-Less!

Then we walked over a red, bare hill to the boarding school. There it sat looming, a large stone structure. I was carrying a small box of red plums we had picked on our way out of the canyon. Just as we reached the school compound, I tripped and fell headlong on my belly, and the plums rolled everywhere. What a sight I must have been.

Inside, I was given a number—37—which was written on all my clothes in large bold numbers. I clutched mom's thick layer of skirts and peered at this mean-looking woman marking my clothes and giving orders. Before I was taken to be with the rest of the children, mom took me aside, "Go my child, go to school," she said. "It's the very best thing you can do for yourself. You know I never went to school. As a result, I am not able to give you the kinds of things you need to make your life easier. I have taught you well. Remember that." With that she hugged me closely, and she and dad left. Tears I tried to hold back ran down my face as the dormitory matron led me away.

LEARNING TO READ

At the boarding school, I discovered my love for language. I was intrigued by what the adults around me were doing—jotting things on paper, giving it to someone, the other person looking at it, and responding. When Ashkii, my grandson, was two or three, he used to sit on my lap and watch me read. He would look up at my face, trying to see what I was doing that seemed to have my whole interest. Learning to read and write in English came easily for me. Because I was so curious about what others were doing, I began taking books and naming letters in sentences aloud. I thought that was reading and did so for a long time until an older girl at the school dashed my enthusiasm.

One day, I was sitting by a window voicing letters aloud again when she sat by me. "What are you doing?" she asked. Proudly, I responded, "Reading!" "That's not reading, stupid, you don't read like that," she laughed. Then she ran off to tell the rest of the big girls, and they all laughed about me. I was always the butt of that joke after that.

In their attempt to ridicule me, I like to think that these girls did me a great favor, for I immediately set out to find out what reading was/is. There was a Navajo teacher who taught "Beginners", those of us who were in school for the first time. I told her my dilemma, and though she knew I had not really learned to sound out all of the letters in the alphabet, she patiently explained what reading was about. "When you learn all the sounds and can put them together, they will convey what you are thinking and what you want to say. Don't worry, you will learn to read," she promised. Because I was so eager to learn to read, I worked hard at doing so, and was able to read short passages of the Dick and Jane series by the end of that school year. Without meaning to brag, I surpassed most of the kids in my class and continued to do so in matters of language after that. Of course math was a whole different story; I will not go there.

As you know, our culture does not have a formal system of writing. What it had and continues to have are the symbols we weave into our rugs, paint on our potteries, draw into our sand paintings, and etch into rock walls to pass on the history of our beginning and our teaching. However, the dominant society does not recognize this as a form of writing. Black on white is what distinguishes what they consider writing from all others. As a result, there were no books or paper for reading in my mother's household when I was growing up.

After I learned to make meaning out of combining words, I attempted to read writings on food items mother bought at the trading post. I distinctively remember "Blue Bird Flour" and "KC Baking Powder." One summer day, I found a frayed, old dictionary at the bottom of a box of clothes some white missionaries had given us. I was so excited by this find. You would have thought I had found a bundle of money or something. I couldn't wait until the afternoon when I was free from herding sheep and helping mother dye wool to get to it.

When I finally got the chance, I poured over that book like it was the last book in the world, and for my world it was. I carried it everywhere, after the sheep, on visits with relatives, and even on our monthly trips to the trading post. I can pretty honestly say, then, that I taught myself to read from this battered dictionary a missionary put in a box bound for the Navajo Reservation.

I sat atop a high rocky formation while the sheep grazed below me and read from the dictionary. Sometimes I had access to a pencil with which I copied passages from the dictionary onto brown grocery bags. Other times, I scrawled passages with a stone on the sheer rock walls of the canyon at Ki'ts'iili. Sometimes mother had to call me several times before I heard her, for I was so engrossed in my language study. I read somewhere about an individual who also taught himself to read from a dictionary. This was Malcolm X who describes how, while in prison, a dictionary set him free.

From that point on, I was to spend nine months out of the year at school, only returning home briefly in the summer. However, mom's teachings have stayed with me and helped me find my way in this world. Though she has been gone for forty plus years, I remember her words as if she spoke them yesterday.

My younger sister also began boarding school in Chinle when she became of age to go to school. She also started at the Chinle boarding school, and later attended the Albuquerque Indian School where she graduated from high school. My older sister was kept at home by mother to help her around the home and to herd sheep until she was eleven years old. Your Aunt/Grandma Betty was a beautiful, tall, slender girl. One day school officials came to take her to school. People had been telling her that this might happen sometime. Upon seeing the cars drive up, she took off running down among the sagebrushes and juniper and hid from them. They didn't get her that day, but eventually they got her and took her to the Intermountain Indian School in Brigham City, Utah. There she learned to be a home service worker under what was called a Five Year Program. Kids who were over-aged were sent on this program. When she finished, she was placed in homes of white people in cities like Salt Lake City, Utah; Denver, Colorado; and Boulder, Colorado to clean their houses and take care of their children. Our younger siblings also started school at the Chinle Boarding School which by then had been moved and rebuilt in another area.

MEETING MY PATERNAL GRANDMOTHER

During one of these trips back to boarding school, I had the occasion to see my paternal grandmother whom I had never seen although I had heard stories of her. She lived deep in Canyon Del Muerto with her medicine man husband, an old, old man named Chaalaa Neez. Her mother had been captured by Mexicans as a young girl, and when she returned two or three years later, she was pregnant. As you older children know, my father and Pa were cousins, but in Navajo they were considered brothers. Their mothers were sisters, coming from the same mother. This grandmother was the product of that pregnancy.

Scrambling up the steep incline and running headstrong into the stone house perched above the orchard, I was stunned by what I saw. There sat a white woman; I could not believe it! On the floor of the hogan sat an elderly woman with her legs extended in front of her, and her hands folded in her lap. Her long while hair hanging loose about her shoulders still had red streaks in it, and her skin was very, very fair. She looked past me with eyes that were completely covered by what I think were cataracts.

HARVEST TIME IN
THE CANYON

Before going to boarding school for the first time, my parents, my sisters, and I used to help my mother's sister and her husband harvest their crops and store them every fall. I remember picking peaches off the trees or picking those that had fallen to the ground and hauling them by the wagon load to a place to be set up to dry. There was a place where the rock wall of the canyon seemed to hang low, forming an overhang, before shooting straight up again. Here we took the peaches, pulled them apart, removed the seeds, and set the halves side by side to dry, safe from the wind or rain. What other peaches my parents could salvage at Standing Rock from passers-by who often helped themselves to unattended orchards, they hauled to her sister's drying place and included them there. The corn, also, had to be husked, dried, and stored in storage pits in the canyon walls. In winter, we made trips into the canyon to retrieve some of it for food.

All summer, Deaf Woman was also very busy preparing wild spinach for winter. She would gather armloads of bee weed leaves and boil them. When it cooled, she took a handful of the deep dark vegetable and slapped it onto rock walls under overhangs where they sat all summer. In late fall, she went about scraping them off and storing them in flour sacks. She re boiled these with mutton fat in winter and it was really quite tasty.

Prickly pear would be just red and ready to burst by now, and winter preparation of food would not be complete without them. After the corn and peaches were stored, we moved to a place called Tse'anoodozi to harvest this fruit. This is just beyond that cave where old *Thin*, mom's grandfather, and another man painted themselves in red ochre high above the canyon wall.

Special tweezer-like prongs were fashioned out of two pieces of wood to pick the fruit off the cacti. When several buckets-full were picked, they were emptied out onto a grassy area. Then they were brushed over and over with a special weed brush until all of the tiny, hair-like thorns were removed. These were so very sweet and juicy that we children ate a bunch before they were brushed well enough, and we got thorns stuck on our tongues. In late September, all the crops would be put up, and it would be time to return to the winter camps above the canyon.

Today, as you know, no one lives in the canyon anymore. With the advent of schools and jobs, people have moved permanently above the canyon to the small communites of Delmuerto and Chinle to be closer to these things. Also, in the 1970's, there was a big scare that the earthen Tsaile Dam situated at the mouth of the canyon in Tsaile was in danger of breaking any day. People were told that if that happened, a wall of eighteen feet of water would come crashing down the canyon. The few people who continued to make their homes in the canyon were ordered to move out. Thus, many home sites and fields were abandoned. Today Tamarisks and Russian Oak have overgrown the canyon floor, and sand piles high from the summer winds, making driving into the canyon impossible. A few orchards and fields continue to be maintained with people walking into the canyon for one day.

GOING BACK TO
SCHOOL ON SUNDAYS

I remember the years of going to boarding school. I especially remember the Sundays in winter when they would drive me back to school in the wagon. Mother would wake me up at about 5:00 or 6:00, and it would still be pitch black outside. She was gentle but firm about my getting up. I jumped out of bed, ran outside, and scrubbed my face briskly with the cold snow. Somehow I dressed in long underwear and outer clothing and hurried through breakfast. The hogan was warm and cheerfully lit by the fire in spite of the cold outside that early in the morning. Breakfast was hot fry bread, mutton stew, and coffee. We ate heartily for the long journey ahead of us. After breakfast, mother bundled me in warm quilts from head to toe, determined that the heat from all the warm food would not escape into the cold morning air.

Mother's quilts were thin and worn. She sewed them by hand often out of flour sacks covering two old blankets. I remember how mom heard the church women of the Delmuerto Church were getting together to sew quilts for Christmas, one year. We had driven our wagon all night from Black Rock toTsaile and all the way around to Delmuerto to be closer to this community for Christmas. While there, mom heard that women who helped sew were to be given quilts. Eagerly, mom went to the church every day to help sew, so she could get a new quilt to cover her children with on those cold winter nights.

At the end of the Christmas program and dinner, quilts were handed out to the women who helped. Patiently, mom sat to be handed her bundle, but it didn't come. When she inquired afterward, she was told she was not a regular member of the church, so the women decided she would not get one. Also, she still practiced the traditional ways of her people. Oh, mother was so disappointed, but she just took it in. I have had no use for that group and their church ever since.

Here were people who were just as poor or poorer than my mother, acting like they were better than her just because of their new found faith and church. They didn't know they were doing the very opposite of the true teaching of that church.

I keep digressing, but there are so many stories within my stories. Shortly, we all piled into the family wagon, which stood ready with the horses hitched up to it. The wagon drawn by horses was our only means of transportation my parents owned. At that time in the morning, the freshly fallen snow was deep, cold, and untouched yet by man or animal. The horses walked with a light step. They were young, healthy, and strong. White breaths of steam like feather plumes flowed from their nostrils. They never slowed their pace, even when the snow and wind were harsh and must have stunned their faces. I buried my face in the thick covers. The road was empty of any people, and I always wondered if I was the only child who had to go far away from home to go to school.

I remembered how warm and glowing the boarding school was after the bleak journey. Mom must have been tired, but she walked straight and proud beside my dad as they escorted me back into the building. Inside, mom always took me aside and gave me some words of wisdom to abide by while away from home. Today, although I am past sixty I continue to be grateful that my parents taught me love, patience, discipline and what it means to be strong. I have always tried to teach my children and grandchildren those same attributes. My older sister was probably off with our father and his family, and my younger sister was not old enough to go to school.

CHILDHOOD MEMORIES

There were many other happy childhood memories of my mother's home in Black Rock that I often shared with you. There is one that I like to remember. Every day in summer, I followed the sheep home at noon on that rutted wagon trail leading to mom's home from the east. A low rumble always sounded from somewhere behind me over the distant mountain. A cool wind picked up and rustled the juniper boughs and sagebrush leaves. The sheep would be long gone, running for the corral as they often did, going home. They usually left a smelly cloud of dust.

I entered mom's round, earthen hogan. There she would sit at her loom weaving and humming her sacred weaving song. She often stopped and greeted me. "You look tired and hungry, my baby. Come and sit by me." I would sit by her and she stroked my tangled head of hair and sang to me a song she had only for me, "Awee'nijool, she yazhi nijool."

A pot of beans would bubble and boil on the sawed-off barrel stove in the center of the hogan. There was no furniture. Our dishes, utensils, and our food sat in wooden crates stacked on top of one another. Our sheep skin beddings were folded neatly against the walls. My younger brothers and sisters would run in and out, laughing as they chased one another. Mother chided them for running and yelling before a rain storm. The floor was bare with no carpet or rugs—just cool, red earth. Over head was an interweaving of logs around the black smoke hole, the only opening.

Soon the rain reached us, and the kids came inside and sat down. We enjoyed beans with hot tortillas on the floor. Those were the good old days when life was a joy with mother there.

Of course there were sad times, too. What I consider the saddest was when mother went away and did not come back for many days. When I was about seven or eight, we lived in Canyon Delmuerto at Kits'iili with our Naaliis, Yazzie and Angelo Clark. One morning I watched my mother ready to go somewhere as she prepared hot tortillas and fried potatoes for breakfast. Her hair bun was freshly made, and she had on her better skirt and blouse.

It was clear she had been up for some time. My younger brother and sister were just waking up and rising from their covers on the ground. This was our humble abode at that time, a brush arbor with just our bedding, a couple of wooden crates to hold our dishes and food, and a wash basin stand at the door way.

There was a hurriedness in her voice and movement as mother chided us through the meal, washing our few utensils and hanging them up in a flour sack from one of the overhead beams of the roof. Soon the kids ran out to play. Mother stopped me from whatever I was doing and stunned me with what she had to say. "My baby, my child," she said, "I have to go away. There is something terribly wrong with me, and I have to get help. I don't know when I'll be back, or if I'll be back. I don't know what it is, but I am very afraid of it. Please take care of your brother and sister. Your naaliis are here and will be able to help you."

Before I could digest what she had said, she walked off, heading westward, carrying a small bundle. "Shima!" I cried and ran after her, "Shima!" She didn't look back but kept on walking. I stood there crying and yelling after her. It did no good for soon she walked over the rise and was gone. Today, I think she must have cried too as she walked away. I know I would have for leaving my babies behind and not knowing what outcome lay ahead, or if I would ever see them again. However, in order for her to help herself, this was a sacrifice she had to make. Our father must have been away working on the railroad, for he wasn't there, and my sister Betty was probably visiting her father and his family.

Days passed and we got by the best we could. As an eight year old, I tried to understand what was going on. When what little food mom left us ran out, our Naalii shared her meager food with us. The Naalii man was always on the go, so he was one less mouth to feed. Every day we looked toward the way our mother went, hoping to see her there, walking back over the rise, but she never came.

One day a pickup truck drove up. We all jumped up and stood at the doorway of our lean-to. Back then there were not very many vehicles around. One man and his wife were the only ones with a truck. From around the other side of the truck came our mother, smiling happily. She scooped us up in her arms and embraced us warmly. We held one another and cried.

Days later, mother took me aside again and related the difficulty and fear she had lived with for many months. She said she was treated at the clinic in Chinle and was now okay. The problem was not what she had feared. Our mother returned to us, and we spent many more happy years with her before she died.

MY FIRST
ROMANTIC ENCOUNTER

I indicated early on how certain scents remind you of things that happen in your life. Well, whenever it rains in Tsaile or Black Rock, the deep pervading scent of damp earth mixed with the pungent sagebrush, juniper, and pinon reminds me of my first romantic encounter. When I was twelve I met a young soldier boy. My family was co-sponsoring an Enemy Way Ceremony, and we had taken the staff to White Clay on a cold, rainy day. Shortly before nightfall, two guys walked up to the truck I was sitting in, selling an assortment of goodies for an aunt. After they bought a can of Skoal, they continued to stand by the truck making small talk. Soon one walked off while one remained. I learned they were on Leave from the Air Force and were due to leave early the next morning.

The young man and I sat on the tailgate of that truck and talked throughout the night. I don't remember what we talked about. After all, what do two young people attracted and fascinated by one another talk about? However, we did promise to keep in touch by writing. All too soon, the other guy was back reminding his friend it was time for them to leave. The last I remember of that soldier boy was watching him walk away into the early misty dawn. I never saw him again, but whenever, I get a whiff of this particular scent, my mind goes whirling back to that long ago night, and I am twelve years old all over again.

GOING TO BORDER TOWN SCHOOLS

After about four years at the Chinle Boarding School, we were called together and informed a bus would be leaving to take students to a place called Snowflake to continue their schooling. We were instructed to tell our parents and get their permission to go. When my mother came to visit me again, I told her about it, but she said she didn't want me to go far away to school too. "Your sister is already far away in Utah. Wait until next year when you are also a little older, she said.

However, before the year was up, I was being transported to the Snowflake Border Town School in a jeep over dirt road. The road between Chinle, Ganado, Steamboat, and the Keams Canyon Junction was not paved yet. We drove all day and arrived in Holbrook at sun down. The driver deposited me at that border town dormitory where I stayed. Very early the next morning we left there and arrived in Snowflake about noon. Mom never came to see me there, but I was able to return home for summer breaks.

At Snowflake, we stayed in some kind of metal buildings at night and attended the Snowflake Grade School during the day. I had never seen so many white children all at one time and in one place before, and that was the first time I attended school with them. The thing that stands out in my mind about the school here is one teacher, a very pleasant white woman. From the very start, she catered to me, more than the other Navajo students in class. In the few years that I had been in school, I had already started leaning toward reading and writing. Math was so very hard for me, though. In my second year, I remember she assigned a paper, and a Mexican girl and I did exceptionally well at it. She praised us up and down and reprimanded the white students. "English is a second language for these two girls, and they did so much better than you who have been speaking English all your lives," are the words that I still remember today. Certain people and situations gave me the incentive to excel as a little girl, and this woman's praise was one of them.

While at the Snowflake dormitory, we were also bussed to another small town up the road to go to school. I went one year and do not have fond memories of it. Mr. B was our home room teacher and sometimes he went away. When this happened he always asked this one man I will call Ch'iidi (Devil) to take his class. We Navajo girls abhorred him! Oh my God, there he was again one morning, standing at the door grinning from ear to ear. My heart just sank to the ground. Mr. B had not told us he was going to be gone today. My palms began to sweat and tears formed in my eyes. What's he going to do to us today? Shall we just leave and walk three miles back to the dormitory where we'd also be in a lot of trouble? The last bell had just rung, calling all students to class.

Devil was an ugly man with blonde hair. His bulging red eyes usually gleamed hungrily when he looked at us Indian girls. Monday was our first encounter with him. God, what a day that was! Long whisker-like hair stuck from his bushy eyebrows and out of his nose. The tip of his nose was always red, and he had large pink hands. The minute we walked in, his eyes lit up, and he cackled in a nasty way and rubbed his hands together. I felt like a helpless lamb when a coyote got too close to my mother's herd and snatched one away. I was so scared that I shook.

Class began. All the time he seemed to be circling his prey and licking his chops, knowing that soon he was going to have his way. MY GOD! What was I going to do? I thought of his hot, clammy hands on me yesterday, and I hated it. How I hated it! I wanted to yell and scream, but who would believe me? It was like a nightmare where I wanted to yell and move, but I couldn't. Music class began, and I tried to sing, but I couldn't get into it. Here it was my favorite class. I sat there with this impending doom hanging over me. The Devil kept looking at us. There were three of us Navajo girls in a class of all white boys and girls.

Loudly the bell rang, announcing recess. He let the rest of the class out, locked the door, and started for us. We were just stunned as we stood rooted to one place. Once one of my sheepdogs and I suddenly came upon a small rabbit. It was so startled that it just sat there, unmoving, with its ears laid back. At that instant, I was that rabbit. However, one of us came to our senses and took flight, and the other two followed. For five minutes or so, we raced around the long, brown, wooden tables, crawled under them, and climbed over them. When he caught one of us, his ugly hands were all over that unfortunate one. The other two of us huddled in the corner holding one another. What a sickening and disgusting feeling that was. I still shudder today, when something happens and I think of this incident. But this went on for a few weeks, and then he stopped coming. We didn't see him again in school. I honestly wished he had died and gone to HELL!

Many years later, after I had married and had children, I was attending a reading conference, and whom should I see but this hideous man. The Devil was very much alive! Do you know what he was doing? He was advertising and selling children's books. He was still in operation! I was so afraid he would see and recognize me, so I ducked behind a screen. He was older, of course, which made him even uglier. There were that demonic grin and bulging eyes. I found the nearest bathroom, threw up, and left the conference.

I have never confided this terrible ordeal to anyone, especially my family. This is the first time I'm putting it on paper. Today there are all kinds of laws and rules about people like this, and applications are supposed to be screened carefully for people that will have anything to do with school children, but somehow they get through the cracks. Take care of yourselves out there.

MISSION SCHOOL
AND ENCOUNTER
WITH PEYOTE

After Taylor, I arrived at Ganado Mission High School in the eighth grade. This was a Presbyterian school. A missionary man whom I used to baby sit for in Chinle encouraged me to attend this school, even paying the first year's tuition for me. Following that, I always stayed on campus in the summer to work for my tuition until I graduated. The thing that sticks out in my mind today about this school is a large sign at the entrance way of the school: Tradition, the Enemy of Progress.

I became indoctrinated into the Christian faith while there. Every Sunday I went out with a missionary couple preaching to the community that the traditional ways, the ceremonies and teachings of the Navajo were works of the Devil. In spite of this, I had my share of rebelliousness as a teen. My friends and I were always sneaking off campus to attend country dances in nearby towns, especially in summers. We even tried to learn how to smoke under a juniper tree at the edge of the grave yard. After coughing up a storm, we buried the cigarette right there until we returned to it the next day to continue. Years later, I wondered why I was having trouble breathing.

One night I woke up in my dormitory room from a dream I was having while at Ganado Mission. I had been dreaming of an object I had never seen before. However, I was very comfortable with it, as if I had known it all along. The object was a tiny, conical shaped thing that was narrow at the top and wide at the bottom. The top was white and the bottom was green with white spots. I lay awake for a long time trying to figure out what

I had just dreamed about. A wide moon beam also flooded into my room through the window on the west side. At some point, though, I turned over and went back to sleep. I never gave the dream another thought until five years later, when I came face to face with the object of my dream.

All my life, I had heard about a ceremony where people ingested a plant that made them do crazy things. As children, we were severely forbidden to go near such gatherings. People were said to turn the lights off as soon as they ate the plant and engage in some sort of sexual orgy all night long. I did not know what plant these people were eating, but later I learned it was Peyote. "People will give you some of that plant, and you will go crazy!" we were constantly reminded, and we were very afraid.

One evening after we had been married a year, your Chei Lee returned from work and asked me to go with him to a peyote meeting. He explained to me what it was and the activities that take place in it. I agreed to go with him more out of curiosity than anything else. The meeting was at Black Rock, not very far from my mother's home. After picking up your Uncle/Chei Harry and Grandma Evy, we drove out of Chinle. We arrived at the meeting place just as night was falling. The peyote meeting had just started.

Gathering our blankets, we followed a man that came out to meet us and sat down on the north side of the hogan. After getting situated comfortably on the ground, I looked around at the people that sat around the circle of the dwelling. I recognized a few from the local area, but most of them I did not know. A man sitting directly in the middle on the west side was smoking a cigarette and speaking or praying. I did not know him, but he somehow appeared to be in charge of things. Just then I focused on a mound of dirt fashioned in the manner of a crescent moon in the center of the hogan. Right smack in the middle of the moon sat that conical, green object of my dream from five years before! I was stunned! I looked around nervously. My heart began to pump fast, and I broke out in a sweat. 'What could this mean, and how could this be happening?' I wondered.

Shortly, we were passed corn husks and tobacco that we rolled and smoked, which made me cough up a storm like I did when I was trying to learn to inhale back at the mission school. Then we were given hard, dry things that looked like dried peaches we used to set out to dry in the canyon at harvest time. I looked uncertainly at my husband who said this was medicine and for me to chew it and rub it on my body. It was very, very bitter, unlike anything I had ever eaten in my life. People sang, shaking a rattle while a man beat a drum for them. This went round and round the

35

hogan. Meanwhile, the man in the middle on the west encouraged people to pray by rolling a cigarette or with a handful of dry cedar leaves. Now and then the bag of peyote was passed, and people ate freely from it.

Before the medicine took effect on my mind and body, I was wondering when the man on the west was going to give the order to have the light extinguished. I was afraid. After awhile, though, I began feeling very calm, and that same sensation of well being and comfort I experienced back in my dormitory room, washed over me again. I did not try to resist the medicine but allowed it to take full control of my body, and I became fully relaxed. I learned more about myself as a woman, a Navajo woman, the mother that I would soon be, and the grandmother that I would one day be that night than at any other time in my life. I broke down and wept for the opportunity to experience the peyote way and all the wonderful things of life this herb would offer and open to me if I chose to follow it. Every negative thing I was told about it as a child was simply not true. All I witnessed that night were singing and praying for the good of the people.

At dawn, a woman carried a bucket of water into the hogan and prayed over it. Then what I know today as the ceremonial breakfast (corn, fruit, meat) was brought in for all to eat. Following that and after a few words of encouragement were shared with the sponsors of the meeting, we left the hogan to go out to greet the new day. I felt very light and happy. 'What an accomplishment', I thought, for even though I was seven months pregnant, I was able to sit on the ground for ten to twelve hours.

Today, partaking of peyote/medicine and praying with it is my whole way of life; I cannot imagine life without it. Since that first experience, your Chei/Lee has become a Peyote Roadman, praying for sick people or for people who want prayers for their children's birthdays, education, birthings, to excel at certain functions that they undertake, or just to live good, prosperous lives. Every weekend finds us at someone else's home, and I am bringing in water at dawn and praying over it. Literally, we have grown up with this way of worship, for we began conducting meetings in our early twenties after Lee's father who was also a roadman, passed away. Through this way, your grandfather and I have tried to bring you up. We do not wish for any other way.

GRADUATING FROM HIGH SCHOOL AND RELOCATION PROGRAM

Getting back to the history of my schooling, I graduated from Ganado Mission High School. Only Grandma Betty came to my graduation. She brought a set of white luggage for me to carry my meager belongings home. Mom was in the hospital right there in Ganado giving birth to Auntie/Grandma Weeddaa. Betty said she left the other kids home alone in Canyon Del Muerto at Standing Rock, instructing them to run to Red Water's house in case of an emergency. She had asked a man from the Presbyterian Church in Chinle to drive her to Ganado for my graduation and to take us home afterward. Mom was not ready to be released from the hospital yet. Thus, we returned home, walking the rest of the way from Chinle.

Before graduating from high school, we seniors were given some kind of test by the Navajo Tribal Scholarship Committee. It was to see who was "college-material" and who was not. A few of us showed we were not by failing the test. Forty was the passing mark and I made 39. I remember how happy everyone was, excited to be going to college. They were asking one another to be roommates.

The principal of the school was devastated for me. One day he took me to the scholarship office to try to coax the officials to change their minds. "You're a bright student and have been on the honor roll all the time you have been here. You deserve to go to college," he said. He was right; other than math, every subject I took came easily for me in high school. Of course, I exerted a lot of effort and worked hard to be where I was; I enjoyed learning. He pleaded with them to rescind their decision, but they would not budge. I remember the words of one of them, "If she can't make it in high school, how do you expect her to make it in college?"

With college out of the question for me, I returned home and applied for the Relocation Program. This program was one more attempt of the US Government to assimilate Native Americans into mainstream America. Whatever its aim, It gave me a start in life. I was accepted for a Licensed Practical Nurses training program in Dallas,Texas.

GOING ON RELOCATION

My mother, bless her soul, had a Blessing Way Ceremony performed for me before I left to embark on this part of my life's journey. This, you know is the proper thing to do when a child is going away for a certain length of time. As soon as the last song of the ceremony was done at dawn and a little breakfast, my Pa and I left, heading for Chinle. We needed to get there in time to meet the driver that would take me to the bus depot in Gallup. I rode a horse while Pa walked alongside. A blanket of snow covered the ground that November morning, as I left my mom and the home I would never really return to except in short spurts. We traveled to the rim of Canyon Del Muerto, down the Blue Spruce Trail, on the canyon floor, up the Twin Trail, and finally to Uncle Hoskie's hogan in Delmuerto. He had killed a horse the day before, and he gave us warm horse broth. After a long tiring journey, we enjoyed the broth. Early the next morning, we hitched a ride to the Chinle Sub Office.

I remember riding the Greyhound Bus for two days and arriving in Dallas at night. I had been given a piece of paper from the Chinle office, instructing me to go to a specific hotel when I arrived at the bus depot. A cabbie who must have seen my bewildered state approached me and asked where I wanted to go. I gave him the paper. He looked at it and said, "This is no place for a young girl like yourself. Let me take you to the Y." The next morning, he even came back for me and dropped me off at the Relocation Office in that city. I guess not all men in strange cities have wicked ideas about lonely girls as shown on TV.

At any rate, I trained for one year and then I worked for a year at the Methodist Hospital. While I was working, I took classes for Pharmacology which enabled me to administer medication to patients as an LPN. During this time there was still a lot of segregation going on. While at Methodist, there were separate water fountains for "Coloreds" and "Whites". There were also different eating areas. "Coloreds" were not allowed to eat in the hospital cafeteria. They ate in a long, smoke filled hall. Because I had more friends among this group, I used to eat with them until one of my instructors led me away to the hospital cafeteria one day. So I guess I was considered White. I liked the dark hallway, though, for there was more laughter and happy atmosphere. The thing that surprised me most was how Blacks were not allowed to attend the State Fair the same day the Whites went. I found this to be very strange.

RETURN TO RESERVATION AND MARRYING MY LIFETIME PARTNER

I always knew I would return to the reservation one day, so when the man who was responsible for my being in Dallas wrote and said there were openings for nurses at the Chinle Health Center (clinic), I applied and got a job. At the clinic I was given a place to live in government quarters.

When I reported for work Monday morning, I ran into a classmate who had also not passed the scholarship test two years earlier. She was working as a receptionist in one of the departments. As we reminesced about high school, she informed me that everyone who passed the test and went off to the university had flunked out in the first semester. She further related that one of the other girls who had not passed the test either went to a college prep school in Phoenix for a year. This girl would later go on to graduate from a college in the east where her adoptive white parents sent her. She would also direct a school on the reservation and write a book.

I believe the Navajo Tribal Scholarship Committee did me a terrible disservice. They denied me the opportunity to go to college at a younger age when my mind was fresh and very eager to learn. I always wondered what I could have made of myself, and how much higher than the MA that I eventually earned I could have gone. However, I decided at that time I would not waste my time bemoaning what could have been. I had a wonderful life with a loving husband, three great children, and five adorable grandchildren. I would never have exchanged them for anything.

Not too long after I returned to Chinle, I met your Chei, Lee. Back then, chapter house dances were very popular with one going every weekend. Local bands made up of Navajo men and boys sang country/western songs and these dances were the "in" thing. Dancing to live bands continues today, but the old chapter house dancing is gone. He was a very nice looking young man, tall and slender and a star basketball player for the Chinle High School. When I tell this fact to my grandchildren today, they exclaim, "No way, not grandpa!" At any rate, mother did not sit still when she learned I was seeing a young man. Rather than leaving it to the family to ask for me to marry their son, she took it upon herself to do so. She went to see them and even set the date for the traditional wedding, February 27, 1967.

I think she saw something good and decent in Lee, and was not going to let him get away. Indeed he has proved to be a wonderful man and husband. He has never ever been rough with me or pushed me around in the forty years I have been married to him. Once at the hospital a nurse taking my history asked if I felt safe at home. Her question took me by surprise, for why wouldn't I feel safe? Of course I felt safe! Just as quickly, though, I realize how some women have to live with fear, violence and abuse, and that was what she was referring to. Wow! I have always bragged that God created my husband and then threw away the mold.

Navajo Community College had opened in Many Farms and was offering classes at the new government high school there when I returned to the reservation to work at the Chinle Health Center. It was awaiting construction of its brand new campus at Tsaile. Your uncle or grandpa Brent was a year and half when your aunt/grandma, Leigh Ann was born during this time.

MOVING OFF
RESERVATION

Lee's apprenticeship in Plumbing and Pipefitting took him to Phoenix, so I asked for a transfer to the Phoenix Indian Medical Center after receiving my ten-year pin at the Chinle Health Center. The old relocation era that was responsible for my going to nurses training in Dallas was coming to an end at this time. The last thing it did for us was buy us a home in West Phoenix off the Black Canyon Freeway. After getting situated in the city, we came back for our children who were staying with their grandparents, Jack and Lula To'aheedliinii. Brent was three and Ann was one and half. Because they had stayed with their grandparents all this time, they got a good, solid grounding in Navajo in the early years of their lives. And I believe we hurt the old couple severely when we more or less snatched the kids abruptly from them.

They did not know any English when we took them to Phoenix. On their first day at day care, Brent met the first Black kid and was just astounded by his thick, kinky hair. When we went to pick them up after work, he couldn't help but touch the Black boy's hair. He ran his hand over it saying, "David Yaan," and ran past us out the door. The little boy's name was David Young. We waited until we were in the car to laugh at what Brent did. The kids were excited about living in Phoenix, and Lee enjoyed it as well. I, however, just could not get used to the rat race of the city. I missed the wide open space of the reservation where I could look out and see for miles.

After three years Lee's job took him to Page, Arizona. The huge power plant was being built, and by now he had turned out as a journeyman plumber and pipefitter. We sold our home, bought a single wide mobile home and had it moved there. I resigned my job at the hospital because the nearest Indian hospital was Tuba City, eighty miles one way from Page, and I didn't want to drive that every day. For the first time I stayed home and Lee supported me and the kids.

Brent started school here. That morning I drove him to the school, took a picture of him at the door, and I walked him into the school building to the door of his classroom where his teacher greeted us. His very first teacher was Mrs. Ward. Tara was born at the Tuba City Hospital while we lived in Page. When she was one, we returned to Chinle. The Chinle Hospital was being built and Lee went to work there. Ann started school at the old Kindergarten Center with Mrs. Begay. Two years later, I enrolled Tara at the Kii Doo Baa' Day Care Center in Chinle and began at the Navajo Community College. By now, it had moved to its new campus at Tsaile.

GOING TO COLLEGE

Two years later, I graduated from Navajo Community College with an AA degree in Elementary Education on a grant called Bilingual and Bicultural Program. That fall, I went to work with what was called the Directed Studies Program at NCC teaching reading, writing, and arithmetic to students who had little or no background in these areas.

At the time, also, the Navajo Teacher Training Program was in full force. It financed the education of Navajo students to study at the University of Arizona in Tucson and return to the reservation to teach Navajo children. The tribal administration in office at the time made a directive that by a certain time Navajo teachers would be in classrooms across the reservation. I joined this program and earned a Bachelors degree in Elementary Education. Of course, I continued to work full time at NCC and earned my bachelors degree part-time and in the summers.

Following this, an internship program had begun at NCC. It was a Master's program to train Navajo individuals to teach English to students at the college. The English department felt that students might learn to write better if they were taught by Navajo teachers who shared their educational backgrounds. Four people were all ready in the program when the chair of the English department came to recruit me. I jumped at the offer, for here was my chance to finally do something. That tiny seed of wanting to do and learn more that had lain dormant all these years would finally be allowed to sprout and grow. This was my dream that had been denied me come true.

Thus began my internship at Northern Arizona University where we found a program that seemed tailor made for me called, Teaching English at a Two Year College. I stayed at NCC and team taught with one of the writing teachers in the fall, but in the spring, I up rooted my children and moved them to Flagstaff to begin my course work in graduate studies. I felt if I really wanted this, I would have to make some sacrifices. You know the Navajo concept, T'aaho'ajit'eego. Well, I applied it here.

Lee was working at the Joseph City Power Plant at that time. Brent and Leigh Ann were very unhappy about this arrangement, especially Brent that after a while, I let him come home and go to school in Chinle. Your Grandmother/Aunt Weeda came to live with us one spring. While I was studying at NAU, I drew a stipend from the college.

Brent graduated from high school the same year I graduated from NAU with my M.A. in English in 1985. When I walked down the isle to receive my degree, I was the proudest woman in the world. I was the first from my family to receive such an honor. I thought about my dear departed mother and my grandfather before her who were the biggest influences in my life, and tears of joy ran down my face. They had seen this potential in me and had believed in me as a little girl. Of course there was my immediate family, also, who stood by me all the way.

JOINING THE ENGLISH FACULTY AT DINE COLLEGE

That fall, I joined the English faculty at Dine College and began teaching two developmental writing courses and two Freshman English I classes. Much later, I added Introduction to Native American Literature after attending a six week institute on Native American Literature at the Newberry Library in Chicago. Because I was already employed with the college and I had been recruited by the English Department for the Internship Program, I simply stepped into a position that was open in the department, right after graduate school.

Teaching writing at Dine College became my life. It took precedence over everything for the next thirty years. I was often in my office on Friday afternoons, even on pay days, grading papers or preparing lessons for Monday. That was how committed and dedicated I was to something I enjoyed doing and believed in. I set high standards for my classes and refused to lower them for anyone or settle for mediocre work. I challenged my students and many of them rose to it. I asked them to stretch their minds, sharpen their analytical skills, and deepen their understanding of the material at hand so they could talk freely about it. "If you can make it through my classes, you can make it through anything," I often teased them.

When I was going to retire in spring of 2007, the President of the college, Ferlin Clark, asked me to give the commencement address. At first, I was afraid, for I do not usually speak in front of large groups of people. I also thought I would need someone to write my speech, until a colleague indicated I simply talk about my experience at the college, teaching writing. "What worked for you and what didn't?" he suggested. It was smooth sailing after that, and I really did enjoy writing my speech, and it went over better than I expected.

On this beautiful spring day, an interesting thing happened. The sun was shining brightly. A few clouds floated overhead and the wind kicked up a little bit. Soon the few clouds raced together to the south, over the Black Rock Area. They became dark, and a long, low rumble sounded from them. I had just related the history of my Naashgali Dine'e Clan. To me this occurrence had great significance. My ancestors and the holy people had sounded their voice and given their approval for what I was doing here.

You know, I had always said I wanted to leave a mark on the world, and I believe this was it. As I spoke, the crowd sat up and leaned forward to hear what I had to say. I had captivated my audience, WOW! I saw many people wipe tears away and afterward told me that I made them cry. Even back in Chinle, people stopped me and asked if I was the lady that made them cry. I had always tried to teach this to my writing students: grab your audience's attention and hold it; make them want to keep reading your essay.

A former colleague of mine said, "It's your children; you leave your mark through them." I had to tell her, "No! I love my children dearly, yes, but this is different. I want to be able to do something through my own actions and through my own mind." And that was it for me.

MY TRAVELS

Working for Dine College has allowed me to travel to many places for summer institutes and seminars in the states and even abroad. As I indicated earlier, I attended a Native American Literature institute at the Newberry Library in Chicago. Before going here, I had no idea, Native Americans were writing literature. I always thought that was the realm of white people, that they were the only ones who wrote books. BOY, was I given the surprise of my life! I observed shelves and shelves of books, many of them dating as far back as the Quiche Mayas, when they were writing on tree barks. They were so fragile that they could only be read in special rooms, and we could not touch them with our hands.

Another time, I was fortunate to be selected for another institute at the Evergreen State College in Olympia, WA. I met some northwest coast tribes and observed their lifestyles. Two things stand out in my mind about this place. First, we visited a Salish tribe at work in their long house. It was a long, wide house which they said was constructed out of one redwood tree. Can you believe that, a house from one tree? Of course, these trees are very, very tall, spiring high into the sky, a lot of them you cannot see the ends of. The other one was visiting the people in Neah Bay, the extreme northwest of Washington.

I stood on a high rocky cliff forming the shore line of the Pacific and looked down at the ocean crashing on the rocks below. I had just walked through what I was told was a rain forest to get there. A thick fog covered the place and a soft drizzle drenched the vegetation. As I trudged to keep up with my colleagues, I saw how easy it was to take the wrong turn and become lost. I thought this must be how creation looked at its inception. I mean every place is considered holy, but this seemed holiest of holy. There I went with my imagination again.

I felt so inadequate to be in such a place. I felt I was not prepared to be here. I did not have the proper attire or the right gift. However, I did have my corn pollen which I sprinkled out on the ocean our, grandmother, and prayed for my family and myself. In Ofelia Zapata's book of poems, *Ocean Power,* she talks about a group of Indian men being transported and when they come in sight of the ocean, they express the same concern I felt.

The ancestors of the tribe at Neah Bay were a seafaring people, hunting whales for special rituals. Recently they had brought this tradition back, much against the mad outcry of the white citizens of the Washington state. "Save a whale, Spear an Indian," they cried. After that successful hunt, the state forbade it. We met the young men who took part in that hunt. What I found amazing, also, was how they said their ancestors sailed as far away as Hawai'i and brought back brides.

Then I returned to the Newberry for a two-week session on Tribal Sovereignty. I had always heard about this concept but did not really understand what it meant. The Navajo leaders I asked always just indicated it means the arrow heads and the rainbow surrounding the Navajo Nation Seal. That still did not tell me anything, so when I saw flyers about it, I applied for the seminar, and got accepted. I wanted to find out firsthand what sovereignty was.

I learned Indians have always had what is called inherent sovereignty. No one, not even the U.S. Government, gave it to them. I saw that sovereignty begins with the individual, ME, for example. I am a Navajo woman formally educated in the Western world. I enjoy the numerous conveniences this world gives me: my beautiful, double-wide mobile home; my GMC pick-up truck; my television set and microwave; indoor plumbing; electricity; and the capability to fly in a plane across the Big Water to see new lands and meet new people, and even to go to Chicago.

These things do not diminish my Navajoness, but enhance it. Many of our Blessing Way songs and prayers express how materialistic things like these will come into our paths, and we will walk among them. They even mention we will go among different kinds of people, and what they have, we will be able to obtain. An individual feels positive about herself and is never ashamed of her Indianness. She feels a close connection to the land and everything around her.

When an individual feels good about herself, she is able to carry this attitude over to her children and grandchildren. She teaches the importance of knowing who they are through clanship and know who is related to them. I always told you grandchildren that clanship, the ceremonies, and the language make you unique. When children have a strong cultural and spiritual grounding early in their lives, they succeed better when they get to school. This is our inherent sovereignty.

Education and other things of the white world may take you far away, but things of your culture will always draw you back.When someone, especially a child is going away for an extended length of time, a Blessing Way Ceremony is held. On the second day, a cleansing and purification take place. Sudsy soap from yucca root is prepared for the person to bathe in. Once I heard a medicine man tell a young woman that in her journey outside the Navajo world, she might come upon a body of water or one that is flowing. Very likely, she will see sudsy foam along the shore. "That will remind you of home and this ceremony and beckon you home," he told her. As you know, though, many Navajo children succumb to that glittering world that is so enticing and powerful and do not make their way back.

In reality, I had sovereignty and practiced it all along but didn't know it. I had to go all the way to Chicago to see that. Just like Dorothy in the "Wizard of Oz," Sovereignty was right there in my back yard. I didn't have to look any further than that.

Some of you know that in 1998, I had a chance to go to China. It was important enough to me that I want to share with you some things that I learned there. After all it isn't every day that one gets to China. It was like a dream, very fast paced from day one as we flitted from one end of the country to the other until the tour ended. We visited many places, saw many people, ate many types of food, and did so much. We arrived in Beijing, China about 8:05 PM and it was already Monday night there! We had just left Phoenix, Arizona at 8:00 A.M. that day, and it was only Sunday night back home. I could imagine my family just making their way home. Everywhere on the streets of towns and cities, people rode bicycles with only occasional cars. Our guide informed us that there were 12,000,000 people living in Beijing, and there were about 8,000,000 bicycles.

Day one was spent visiting the China Nationality University, and the Tibet High School. At the university, we were met by four very official looking gentlemen. What struck me about them was they did not speak English. Each had to have a translator. Somewhere I got the idea that English was spoken everywhere, but I learned differently. Here, I learned that China is a country with a large population that just the students of all of China alone matched the population of the United States. The aim of the universities and colleges is to preserve the cultural backgrounds of the 56 minority groups in China. Upon completion of schooling, students are encouraged to return to their specific locales to teach or work in some government capacity.

At the Tibetan High School, we learned students go home only once in three years Many of them we were told traveled 300 miles with their parents to Tibet for transportation to Beijing. My heart went out to these kids to be so far from home. I was already feeling homesick at the time. Apparently, the government finances nine years of their education so they cannot afford to mess around. They have to successfully complete their education and return to Tibet to become leaders of their state. Here, we often think the BIA schools back in the states were harsh. Ours was a piece of cake compared to what the Chinese children have to endure. On the second day, I got to see the Forbidden City, the magnificent site where the traditional Emperors and Empresses lived and carried out their affairs. Remember the movie, "The Last Emperor"? It was filmed here. One thing I did not see at any of the schools we visited was pairing off of couples.

In Salingol of Inner Mongolia, we saw what the herds people lived in. They were round structures very much like our hogans out here. They were called Gers and made out of felt made from sheep wool. While our hogans are stationary, Gers are mobile ready to be disassembled at a moment's notice to move with the sheep. In the process of dinner, we were engaged in a little ritual called, "bottoms up" where a young girl sings to you and hands you a small container of corn whiskey on a silk scarf to drink all at once. Then the scarf was placed around your neck. This is done by the people of the Grasslands to show their appreciation and as a form of greeting. For me, personally, it was the most horrible tasting stuff.

The land here is just unbelievable! Plain grassland expands outward as far as the eyes can see in all direction with a deep blue, cloudless sky above. Not a single tree grows here, just a wide expanse of green hills and flats. I could not begin to comprehend the size of this country. Here, and there, grazed large flocks of sheep. I understood that some people owned as many as 1,000 to 2,000 heads of sheep.

Of all the places we went to in China, this part of the country was my favorite, for it reminded me of home so much. Of course the green rolling hills are absent on the reservation, but the sky is as blue as ever, and the wide open space is there. This land is BIG! Everywhere I looked, I saw a line of sheep moving. Dinner was a mutton feast which really pleased us

Navajos in the group. There was boiled backbone and other bone pieces that we could eat from with our fingers.

At a cultural show that evening, we sat around a bonfire of manure, listening to singing and watching dancing. People there collect cow manure on the grassland for fuel because there are no trees to burn. A group of men squatting off to the side caught my eyes. They were herdsmen come from their camps to enjoy an evening of performances. They reminded me of reservation Navajo men, shabbily dressed and needing haircuts. The Mongolians and Chinese people also have such beautiful singing voices.

Furthermore, I climbed a section of the Great Wall, going about three quarters of a mile to the top. Thunder began to rumble high in the mountain top and the wind picked up. I started back down, hoping to get back to the bottom before the rain came, but that was not to be. Soon large drops began to splat on the stone floor of the Wall. I managed to make it to the second tower from where I turned around before it really began to pour. Thunder crashed and lightning flashed everywhere. Many people ran back down and took refuge under the tower with me. Some were carrying babies and children on their backs. A woman came around selling plastics jackets for five yuwens. We bought some and put them on, for the wind was blowing the cold rain into the shelter. Soon the rain turned to hail and began pelting the Wall floor. When the hail let up, I began walking though the rain was still falling. I was soaking wet by the time I reached the bus. People who rode the cables were nice and dry as they sat on the bus waiting for me. That was quite an experience in a thunderstorm, climbing a part of the Great Wall of China.

The food we were served in China was nothing like the Chinese food we are used to here in the states. There seemed to be so many different types of plants in everything we ate that I thought the Chinese cooks simply went outside their backyard and gathered weeds, and maybe they did. I do not know. I could not stand the variety of spices and seasonings on the food we were served also; they just turned my stomach. I was so afraid of losing my passport, getting stranded in China, and having to eat that food forever. I understood someone finding your passport would only sell it back to you for twenty thousand dollars. We visited the home of the headman in a village one day. On our way out of the house, I looked back and saw a man run out of the yard behind the house with a snake in hand. That was probably lunch.

While in China, my luggage got lost. It did not arrive when we arrived in a province called Kuming. Surprisingly, I did not lose control.

Medication I was taking for diabetes and high blood pressure were in there, as well as my Malaria pills. However, the next day it was found; it had just gotten on another flight.

In Dali, another province, we saw two Pagodas which are tall, spiring structures with plate-like roofs sticking out all the way from the bottom to the top. I understood during an earthquake, the longer one cracked all the way up one side, and it was clearly visible. However, during the aftershock wave, the crack closed up. Here, we also learned that once a year, during a special celebration, people are allowed to take any mate they want, and no one can complain. If you see a woman with your husband or vise- versa, you cannot say anything. I did not know how to take that tradition, just that it was weird. Another time, we saw caves of grottos in the mountains. They were statues of Budda and other deities considered sacred by the people of China. To me they meant nothing, but I respected them for what they represent to the Chinese people.

One day our bus climbed with us up a steep mountain and descended with us on the other side. At the bottom of the mountain flowed a large river, the Yantze. Many farms lined both sides of the river as has been the case everywhere we went in China. I thought the Chinese people are a very hard working people, farming every available piece of land in the country. Many times I saw fields starting right from the side of the road and extending all the way up a mountainside. Everywhere, people are bent over, sitting or plowing. What a hardy people! We visited the Yantze where it bends eastward. We learned that three rivers started from the same source. While the other two flowed straight down, the Yantze made a bend and flowed eastward. Without this bend, there would not be a Chinese civilization. Wow!

We visited the place where the river ran into a narrow gorge and became white and angry, as it roared over huge boulders below. This was Tiger's Gorge, the place where a tiger leaped across the Yantze River to get from one mountain side to the other. Every one went down to the floor of the gorge, but because I have such a fear of water, I stayed on top. I looked down at the high splashing, churning river, heard its loud voice briefly and came away.

Once, our plane couldn't lift off due to heavy rain. I saw fire trucks, an ambulance with lights flashing, and officials lined up on the runway. That scared me, for it meant the flight coming in was in trouble. We didn't fly out that afternoon. I was glad the airline decided to cancel, for just before leaving the states, I had read about the crash of a Chinese plane. On June

17, 1998, we arrived in Banna, a tropical South Asian city. Hot, muggy air engulfed us as we deplaned in this jungle area.

In the mountains of Banna lived the Ani people. Here the people lived in split-level houses. Because the ground was always wet, which caused arithritis, the people built structures on long logs and lived on the top level, using the bottom level for storage. We visited one of the homes. In the center, what would be the west side of our hogans, lay a young man with two stark naked little boys beside him. On the south side sat the hearth where all the cooking was done. To the left of that was a door leading into a small area which I learned was for men's use. I didn't learn what for, though. Another one to the right of the cooking area was for women. There was just the barest of necessities in this home much like mom's hogan I grew up in.

The people here were obviously very poor. Children were very dirty and dressed in rags. Little girls stood around carrying their baby siblings on their backs or hips. Their mothers were by the road above trying to sell some kind of very large mushrooms. The yards were filthy with animals roaming or lying freely on the first level of the home structures. Little girls younger than my seven year old granddaughter, at the time, carried two buckets of water on long metal bars suspended across their shoulders. Today, I wonder if they suffer from rotary cuff tears that I ail from. Many children ran naked. There was a school, where we learned, only the children whose parents could afford to pay for it went to school. Our guide said they get no form of assistance from the government like how our people get welfare back home. And here our people complain when their checks are a little late.

Later that day, we came back down the mountain and headed to a village where we were going to stay for the night. Once more the homes were split-level, but the surrounding was much cleaner. We had to take our shoes off before entering the main house, but that was nothing new to me. Remember, I always made you and everyone else take off your shoes at the door before entering my house? I used to tease that our Tribal President Joe Shirley would have to take his shoes off, too, when and if he ever came to visit. We sat on tiny stools and talked with our host who was the police chief of the village. The wife was busy at the hearth preparing supper. I smiled to myself thinking, these small chairs would be ideal for the Navajo card players back home during Squaw Dances. Shortly we sat down to eat at a small table, using the tiny chairs. We discussed various topics with our host as we ate.

I asked the host if his people had the same problem with drinking alcohol as did my people back on the reservation. He thought a while and then responded that his people were up at dawn to attend to their fields. About noon they returned home to rest for a bit. Then they went back out to the fields until close to midnight. "We just don't have time to sit around and drink," he said. I asked also if there was any form of welfare assistant given to people by the government each month, and he said there was none. The next morning they gave us something called "Sticky Rice" for breakfast. We could scoop out some with our hands, pressed it together, and eat it like bread with a piece of pork sausage between it. It appeared wives and children do not eat with guests but have to wait until the husband and guests were done.

We also sailed up the Mancos River. This river was important because it was used to ship ammunitions to the war by the U.S. during the Vietnam War. The mountains bordering the river on both sides were covered by a thick, green jungle. Immediately, I thought of the Navajo boys who came to fight a war not too far from here. "How many times have they sat on a mountain side and thought of home in this strange muggy land?" I asked myself. Soon it began to rain and thunder crashed loudly. It was a sad instance for me as I contemplated how it must have been for those soldiers, many of whom never made it home. At a botanical park we saw some interesting trees. There was one tree that sought out palm trees with its roots and sucked the life out of them. Then we saw a flower that danced when a melody was sung to it.

The roads in China are very narrow, looking more like alleys. Even on mountain sides, they are like this. Drivers simply honked their horns to warn oncoming traffic that they are driving around corners. There are no markings of any kind. At one place we saw a temple with a statue of Budda sitting in the middle of a room surrounded by statues of lesser deities The white people of our group descended on this temple by taking pictures, asking questions, and looking at this and that. Many minority people of this area came, lit candles, and bowed to the statues. Personally, I felt like we were intruding on someone's private moment with his/her creator/belief.

One day toward the end of our trip in China we left to visit another minority group. Rain pelted an already heavily soaked ground. We headed into a mountain that was drenched. Water poured out of it on both sides of the narrow road and ran deep along the gutters. Cornstalks in fields stood half way in water and rice paddies were flooded. We saw instances where trees were uprooted and mud was starting to slide down into the road. I was terrified, for though I tried not to think about it, I kept remembering news reports where mud slides had pushed vehicles off the road, or flooding had carried cars away.

Seven and half hours later, we arrived in a small town. Since we could not continue our journey due to the rain, we checked into a rinky dink motel. It was so infested with bugs that we had to force ourselves to just even sit on the bed. On the way there, we had seen some white meat in the windows of food shops. We thought they were chicken. To our astonishment, the guide informed us they were butt ends of dogs. He continued to tell us they were adult Pekinese dogs, and people in the area loved eating them. When some of us women went into the bathroom facility of one of the shops, we saw poor, little dogs tied up waiting to be killed.

The next morning we left to visit the last villages on the agenda while in China. Before we began our assent into the mountains, some police officials stopped us. We learned there had been a massive land slide somewhere on the road to the place we were going. Over 20 people had died in a bus like ours and a small car. Wow! What a mind jolter that was. This was exactly what I was afraid of, and that could have easily been us if we had kept on going that first day.

Even after hearing this tragic news, the driver had the gall to suggest we go up a ways before the landslide, so we can see some beautiful sights. Immediately, I thought, 'but how will we turn around?' And I understood the police told him just that, that there would be no way for our bus to turn around. Even then, the guide and driver kept saying, "It'll be alright." These guys were way too daring, caring only about showing some scenery to the white people in our group so they could take pictures. Eventually, we turned around right there and headed back after two of us women voiced our concerns. We learned the road to the very last village we were to see was washed away. I was beginning to wonder, how many more warnings do we need to see what we're up against? Maybe we were not meant to see everything in China. This is a huge country with many mysteries about it.

On our way back down the mountain, we stopped at an eating place. We were exhausted and starving, for we had been driving many hours. We just dove into the first food item we received, which was soup. It was hot and good. Others took seconds, even thirds. When someone asked what it was, we learned it was Eel soup. My stomach sank, for somewhere in my mind I recalled eel is considered a snake in Navajo and is forbidden to eat. Upon consulting with my spiritual advisor back at home, as your Aunt Vicky would say, only a very expensive ceremony will counter the ill effects of it. I don't know, but maybe someday I will have the means to sponsor the ceremony, the Nine Night Male Shooting Way.

Back in Bejing, from where the last leg of our journey home would begin, we took in a Chinese Opera. Beautiful women dressed in colorful attire danced and sang in the show. Later, I learned they were all men dressed in women's dresses. How very much like our Ye'iibichei dancers back home, I thought. In the beginning, dancers were made up of just men. They impersonated female ye'iis. Today, however, girls and woman dance with the men.

We also took the bus and toured the Summer Palace. This is where the Emperor's daughter came to spend her summers. The longest corridor as is recorded in the Guinnes Book of Records can be seen here. I believe it records the history of the Chinese People. There was also a large marble boat that is stationary now, but she sat and sailed on the lake in it. There are so many temples for this and that in China that I lost track and count of them.

On our last day in China, I got up at 5:30, took a shower, dressed for the flight, and ate breakfast. 8:30 was boarding time for the airport, but as usual, certain individuals were late getting on the bus. I thought that on the day we were leaving everyone would be on time. I just couldn't figure this group. Rain was still falling, and this worried some of us, for we had heard that some airlines don't allow their planes to take off in the rain. However, after a long process of getting our luggage checked, our plane did take off on schedule. I got a good seat by the window in the back. A Chinese woman going to Japan sat in the other seat. I enjoyed sipping a cold can of Diet Sprite that I had not had in a month.

On the flight across the Pacific, I sat in the middle row between a white man on the left and an Oriental man on the right. That night, I could not sleep. I tried to read some and watch a movie on TV, but I was too excited at the prospect of going home. I knew night fell, for people went to sleep. I must have nodded off, for the next thing I saw was sunlight streaming in through the window. I couldn't believe it had happened so fast. While eating breakfast of a pastry and coffee at 8:00 A.M., I looked at the watch of the Oriental guy next to me and saw it read 12:00 midnight. I knew that was China time and I continued to be astounded!

China was wonderful and quite an experience, but I was so happy to be back in my hot, dry southwestern home state of Arizona. I know I will never get there again, but I appreciate the opportunity to have gone to China and met many wonderful people and visited such beautiful places in the process. What a dream this has been.

The last place I visited while I was employed with Dine College was Hawai'i. The essay I wrote was picked by the sponsor from among several essays enabling me to go to this island in the western Big Water. The whole time I was there, I felt like I was in a foreign country, and it is, although it is part of the United States. I attended The Hawaii National Great Teachers Seminar on Hawai'i 's Big Island. The highlight of this visit was a huge volcano close to where the seminar took place, an old military base. I learned that this is where the great goddess, Pele, lives. People come to place offerings to her. It was amazing, for her story reminded me of our Changing Woman who went to the western ocean to live. Could they be one and the same deity? The only thing is that Pele had such a violent beginning, while Changing Woman a soft gentle one.

UNUSUAL PHENOMENA

Some unusual things happened in my life that I want to tell you about. I know some of you said that I just had too much imagination while I was growing up. The first thing I remember is how my mother and father went away overnight. They instructed me to take my younger brother and sister over to our Uncle Joe's place when it got dark. He and his wife were also gone off some place, but his elderly mother and father- in- law were home. When we arrived, they gave us some broth and tortillas and took us to our uncle's house to sleep. We lay down on bedding already laid out for us and went to sleep. Later in the night, my younger brother woke me up to take him outside to pee. My sister woke up also and we all went outside. There was a full moon making the night light as day. Shortly, we went back into the house. Before we went back to bed, brother wanted some water. A pail of water sat on the table to the left of our bedding where I gave him a ladle of water, and we returned to bed.

Sometime in the night I woke again, this time to the feeling of something or someone touching my bare, left thigh. I kicked as hard as I could and felt the thing pull back. I was so scared and didn't know what to do. I knew my brother and sister were fast asleep again. I felt carefully for something at the head of our bedding and felt my brother's boot. I grabbed it and threw it as hard as I could at whatever was at the foot of my bed. At this point, I noticed the door was ajar and moonlight pouring into the house. I know I had shut the door when we came back into the house. I heard the thing stir, get up quietly, and to my surprise walk out the door on all fours. It looked like a dog! I bolted for the door and slammed it shut. For a long time, I couldn't still my beating heart as my siblings slept through the whole thing. I never knew what or who happened that night, but as I got water for my brother earlier, I remembered my bare feet touching something furry by the table. Was that thing in the house with us all that time? My parents did not inquire what might have happened, for they thought I was making up the story.

One warm summer morning, when I was about eight years old, another unexplainable event occurred. Mother stopped weaving and asked me to go to the mountain with her to get some cliff rose barks for my infant brother's cradle. Back then these barks were used to line a baby's cradle board. We climbed the steep mountain and found some cliff rose bushes right away. I helped mother strip the barks off the bushes and soon we had more than enough. She stuffed the barks into the flour sack she had brought along for that purpose. "We better get on home; your little brother has probably woken and crying," she said.

Rather than going back the way we came, I wanted to run along the rim of the mountain to the trail that led to our hogan from Canyon Del Muerto. I saw mother disappear behind the thick cluster of pinon trees as I scampered in the other direction. Every so often, I stopped to view the magnificent countryside from that high up. The homes and animals below looked like my miniature clay toys I had constructed to amuse myself during those long, hot summer days. I could see Star Mountain and the Beeshnahaldaas Mountain standing misty blue and ancient far to the east.

As I neared the trail leading down, I noticed something from the corner of my eyes so I turned. There at the edge of the juniper and pinon trees, I saw a woman in a red velveteen blouse with large silver buttons down the front, sitting on a horse. However, I did not look long enough to see who it was. I turned on my heels and ran down the trail, excited that someone was coming to visit us. I was happy because we lived in a very remote part of the reservation where we seldom had any visitors. When I reached home, I could scarcely get the words out to tell mother of the approaching visitor. I was breathless from running and from the anticipation.

Quickly, mother put her weaving aside once more and set about getting a fire started. I could tell she was also eager to receive the visitor to hear some news from the outside. We prepared a meal, tidied ourselves up, and waited for the visitor that never arrived.

To this day, I am still puzzled about who or what I saw that day on the trail. The only access to and from my mother's hogan was the trail on which I saw the woman on horseback. As I think about the incident now, I don't recall hearing any sounds to indicate that someone was riding a horse on the rocky trail. Also, I remember how my mom's late sister was a large woman, and she used to always wear a red blouse with large silver buttons down the front. And this lady on horseback was heavy set and wore that same shirt.

Another very weird thing happened to me another summer. I thought I saw my nephews walking into the woods when they were out with their older brothers driving to the store all that time. The summer afternoon was very hot as we settled down to rest under the huge pinon tree that formed part of the shade for the food arbor. Once in a while, a cool breeze blew down the mountain bordering the camp on the north. Heat waves shimmered in the distance beyond the arbor.

Your grandma Evy was having a Blessing Way Ceremony in Black Rock. The whole family was there with everyone returned home from various cities and towns. Children ran to and fro, yelling and playing, the older kids walked about camp bored, and we parents busied ourselves under the arbor. We had just finished washing all the dishes and putting the food away after feeding the medicine man, the visitors, and the family. Feeling tire and sleepy, I lay down for a short nap.

I must have slept for about thirty minutes when your Chei Lee touched my shoulders gently to tell me he was going back to Chinle. At that point, I became fully awake, so I sat up. My sisters were still sitting at the table visiting and catching one another up on family news. They informed me the guys had gone to the Wilkenson's Store in Tsaile to get some ice.

As I sat on the metal-spring bed which I had been sleeping on, I looked out at the activities of camp. Suddenly, I saw two nephews, one from Phoenix and the other one from Albuquerque leave the horse corral and walk northward toward the woods. I could see they were engaged in conversation, for they were gesturing with their hands and they kept looking at one another. All the kids had been gathering at the corral all morning to pet a Pinto foal, and I assumed they had been there.

After a while, the guys returned from the store. To my surprise, there were the two nephews leaning over the back seat saying something to their brothers in the front of the double-cab Chevy truck. I thought, 'Oh they probably walked through the woods to the main road and caught a ride back with the guys.' I didn't think anymore of it. It wasn't until later that evening that I fully learned all the guys had gone to the store, except for the littlest children. I had asked one of the nephews what he had done that day, and he said he went to the store with Don and Mark. Confused, I responded, "No you did not; I saw you walking around with Trevor." He looked at me oddly as if I was losing my mind and said, "Huh Uh, we all went to the store to get some ice." I was dumbfounded! Whom or what did I see then?

I do not know what it meant to see something like that, especially during a Blessing Way Ceremony. As you know, this ceremony is the granddaddy of all ceremonies there are in Navajo practice. Holistically, we are cleansed and brought back into harmony and balance with nature by it. Nothing out of the ordinary should have occurred during this time. Family members are encouraged to think only positive thoughts and not to argue on this day. However, I also understood how unexplainable events still occur in the 90's and the millennium, for this was a foreshadowing of an unfortunate circumstance that would come in the future. Not everything can be scientifically explained.

Yet another phenomenon happened with Auntie Tanya's and Paul's daughter, Desiree or Dedibei as we all liked to call her when she was a little girl. I don't think her parents will mind if I tell her story here because often you all will want to know what it is we adults are discussing or whom something happened to. I don't want to keep anyone in the family in the dark about anything. I believe this story is important and worth sharing with all of you.

The Tabaahi Clan, Paul's side of the family had come together to celebrate Easter at one of his aunt's place. After dinner, everyone was tired from the huge meal that was consumed and began to slumber off while others bunched up and discussed happenings on the reservation. No one saw Dedibe wander off, but here is what I think transpired:

A smiling boy lingers near with his eyes on a little girl squatting on the ground. Her head is down as she draws lines in the sand and watches sand run through her fingers. As the little girl looks up, their gaze locks. The little boy gestures with both hands and beckons her to come. The little girl smiles, gets up, and follows readily, three quarters of a mile across an empty field. Here they sit down to play near a barbed wire fence. This is where a young man found the little girl, scooped her up in his arms, and carried her home. A spiritual interplay had been interrupted.

In the meantime, an all out search began. People went from home to home, nearby, searching. Some went into the wash looking through trees and calling her name. Neighbors were notified to tie up their dogs that there was a little girl missing, possibly wandering around out there. The parents were frantic and in tears. What had happened to their baby girl? She couldn't just have walked away; it was very unlikely for her to do that.

Some men got into their vehicles and began cruising up and down the roads by the highway. It seemed she had vanished into thin air. Others fanned out across the wide field crisscrossed by barbed wires. That is where the young man found her approximately two hours after she became missing. She was fine, busily talking to herself, it seemed, as she played. You see only Dedibei could see the little boy, no one else. When her parents questioned her, she told them she followed her friend to play with him, and No, she was not afraid.

Medicine people or those knowledgeable in these kinds of phenomena immediately saw this as a divine interlude between spirit and human that Sunshine Boy had manifested himself to visit this little girl. They say encounters like this are common. They suggested spiritual intervention take place through a ceremony before too long. If ignored they said the consequences would not be very good as the child grew that her mind would be greatly affected. Thus, a ceremony ensued, and the little girl was prayed over by many strong medicine people.

This incident reminds me of how on a cold winter night a bear entered the brush arbor of a family of pinon pickers. As they slept, it took their youngest child, a three year old baby girl. My mother, father, and small children were camping with this family when the incident happened. People back then camped in woods far from home to pick pinon nuts to sell to traders. The baby girl had been sleeping between her parents. The mother woke in the night to cover her baby; she felt all around where they were sleeping, but couldn't find her. She became alarmed and woke everyone. The baby was too little to just walk away into the night!

When it became light, a medicine man was obtained and he discerned that indeed a bear had come in the night and taken the baby. He and others performed ceremonies and rituals to appease the bear to return the child. The next day the three year old was found sitting atop a large boulder. No ceremony was conducted for the child after she was recovered, and today the girl is fifty plus years old and suffers heavily from heart ailment.

Sunshine Boy returned to visit Desiree in the summer. Her mother Tanya had gone far away across the Big Water to a country called Switzerland to study architecture. She was seeking to obtain an MA, and a requirement was for her to visit a country to study its architectural designs

One day, Tanya says she found herself in a chapel considered one of the most beautiful structures ever made. Though it was a Christian building, she says it was built by a non-Christian who was inspired by works of nature. He wanted it to be a refuge or haven for people from all walks of life and religion. She said she was feeling particularly sad and homesick that day. Sitting down she began praying in her traditional way, calling upon the Navajo holy people as she had been taught. She called them by name, beseeching each one to please look after her family back in Albuquerque, New Mexico.

Meanwhile her family was sitting down to lunch when Desiree suddenly smiled and got up from the table and made her way out of the kitchen. Paul, her father, was dishing out food onto his daughters' plates when Desiree returned. She continued to smile as she explained, "I told him I couldn't play with him today. I have to go inside to eat. My father and sister are waiting for me." Only she could see Sunshine Boy again, beckoning to her at the door. In the hour of her deepest loneliness for her family, Sunshine Boy answered Tanya's prayer to go and keep Desiree company. However, she did not just follow him unknowingly this time. She knew her place was with her family. Who knows, maybe he'll continue to come around and be her little protector as she grows up.

Today is November 5, 2008, and I'm going to interrupt my story to tell you about the most astounding thing that happened yesterday. The American people voted a Black man into the highest office of the United States of America, that of presidency. No one in their wildest dream thought this would ever be possible. Of course, to us Native Americans a child belongs to the mother's side of the family, and he is what the mother is. In the case of Barack Obama, the President elect, he is white because his mother is white. However, the white officials and newscasters keep saying "…this is the first time an African American has…" That's the way the white people look at lineage, though, which is carried through the father's side of the family. Anyway, this is such a momentous occasion in history that I thought it was worth mentioning here.

Speaking of "firsts," we experienced our own this past weekend. Stephanie went to run in Buena Vista, Virginia, in the United States College Athletic Association's cross country championship. She led her squad to win its first national championship for Dine College. She and three other teammates were named to the women's All American team. Overall, Steph came in fourth among older and veteran runners, which was truly admirable for a first time contender in college. While the girls she ran with in high school chose not to run anymore after high school, Steph accepted a running scholarship from Dine College. We are all so happy for her and proud of her. WAY to GO STEPH!

MY CHILDREN

Now I will talk about my children. You know I have one son and two daughters. Brent was born in the fall of 1967 at 2:09, amid a homecoming parade with the Window Rock High School Band playing in full force. I always thought that that is why he went on to minor in music and enjoyed traveling with the Navajo Nation Band, playing the tenor saxophone for them since he was in the ninth grade. At NAU, too, he played with the marching band and got a chance to travel with it. My son also liked other finer things in life like drawing, writing, and creating native crafts, entering them and winning prizes with them. Often he sat in deep thought, and I wondered what he was thinking about. "A penny for your thought son," I would ask. Academically, Brent excelled in most any subject he took. He was a superior student.

Brent had the gift and mind for the traditional way of living, embracing it wholeheartedly at a time when not very many young people his age showed interest in it. He was fortunate in that he grew up around elderly grandparents who instilled in him the importance of the old way of life and taught him everything he knows. They took care of him from infancy at the sheep camp in Taayilk'id while Chei Lee and I visited him only after work. One winter night we visited again, and we saw grandma had set out a row of bottles of milk for the orphaned lambs. At the end sat a baby bottle for my son. After she fed all the lambs and put them down for the night, she turned to my son. She changed his wet diaper, tied him up securely in the cradleboard, fed him, and put him to sleep. This was her routine every night.

The elderly couple was simply delighted with their great grandson, especially the man who slept with the baby in his arm when he was not sleeping in the cradleboard anymore. Grandpa Jack called Brent Bohii from the start because of Brent's chubbiness. It turned to Ashkii Boh as he grew older, but Bohii has stayed with him throughout his life. Some community people know his as that. The winter of Brent's birth was when the big snow came. It snowed and snowed for several days; people were trapped in their homes unable to get out. To get formula to our son and food to the elderly couple, Lee and I drove to the turn-off from the highway toward their home. There they met us on a horse drawn sled with Brent bundled in a goat skin. We held him, loved him and played with him for a while, and then they took him back. People still refer to the winter of 1967 as the time of the Big Snow.

Today Brent is forty-one years old, but I came very close to losing him one time. I do not like to think about that time, but I think it is important to tell it here for future generation. The very first time I sat at a computer to write down this story, tears came to my eyes and I cried as I typed it.

On a late summer afternoon, of August 11, 2001, I received devastating news from my sister Weedaa that my son had fallen into Canyon De Chelly somewhere. I always thought that if something bad was going to happen, there should be some sign to indicate it. However, I felt nothing. Here, in Chinle Valley, nothing was out of the ordinary just your typical summer day. Lee, Tara, and Terry had driven to Lukachukai. The way ten years old Stephanie came running out of the house, waving the phone and shouting, "Grandma, telephone! It's Grandma Weedaa!" made me feel something heavy and cold deep inside. I whispered, "Oh No!" to myself. I believe that was my warning sign. My heart quickened and the whole world seemed to stand still as I listened to Weedaa relate how Brent had fallen into the canyon somewhere over in the Deez'a area. She didn't know how far he had fallen though. Tears welled in my eyes, and I felt so alone and helpless. I thought of my son so alone somewhere and whether or not he was conscious.

Somehow I regained my composure and wiped my eyes. This was no time for me to break down and cry. I had to get to my son. I told Wanda Bear who was living with her mother that summer what had happened and to watch the kids while I went to see about my son. Weedaa and Marco drove me toward the Black Rock area for the incident had occurred on that side of the canyon rim. In the meantime, Chei Lee and the others had been notified, and they were headed in the same direction. All the way to Tsaile, we followed a rescue unit. By now everyone including the police and health care providers had picked up on the incident and were discussing it as we listened in on the radio. I heard someone say, "He's alert and a nurse is with him." I was bewildered, for the Deez'a part of Canyon De Chelly is very remote. No people lived there this time of the year, and I had no idea who the nurse was and where he/she came from. I was relieved, though, to hear someone was with him. We also learned an ambulance had gone in but was detained at the Tsaile Lake due to the muddy road from there on.

By the time we arrived at the lake, night had fallen. Overhead, the sky was very overcast, threatening more rain. I saw EMT's with huge packs on their backs jump out of the ambulance and head for the rescue truck as it pulled up. From there on, the going was rough over a muddy, dirt road. We followed signs and markers left by people to guide us to the incident site, about ten to twelve miles south of the lake. Jackets were flung over bushes and twigs of juniper were strewn on the road. A police panel and several trucks were parked on a rocky incline. Immediately, the EMT's and the rescue crew gathered their gear and headed down the rocky slope toward the canyon rim, led by one of the police personnel. We were told the rim was about a mile away. All the people I was with followed too.

I followed for a while, but they were too fast for me. The night was very black, and I didn't have a flashlight. Shortly, I just sat down and wept. Now was time for tears, to release all the pent up feeling that had formed like a ball in my chest. I prayed like I had never prayed before that my son would be all right. A cold wind blew out of the west, and a light sprinkle began to fall. Once more I wondered if my son was covered and protected from the elements. Across the canyon on the south rim, I could see headlights of cars moving back and forth. They seemed so close, but I knew a deep chasm separated us. Except for the sound of the wind, the night was absolutely still

After what seemed like an eternity, I heard sounds of voices and feet moving fast over rocks. We had arrived at nine-thirty, and now it was twelve thirty. Six men carrying a stretcher moved past me and everyone else that had gone down to the rim followed. I touched Chei Lee's arm and asked how our son was. He looked at me, and even in the night, I knew he was very afraid. "I think he's alright; he's awake," he said, more to set my mind at ease. Back at the police panel, I touched my son's face lightly. His head and neck were secured in a makeshift brace or splint, fashioned out of an old cowboy boot, and his body was tied down onto the body splint on the stretcher. Because the stretcher did not fit the police panel or the rescue unit, my son was transported out in the bed of Uncle Chet's pickup truck as far as the lake where the ambulance was. Tara and Terry sat with him in the truck bed.

Shortly, the people that had kept Brent comfortable came in. It seems after Brent fell, his brothers went for help, leaving one of them behind. They stopped the first truck they met, which just happened to be driven by a nurse who lived in Black Rock.

Grandma Alice, Aunt Cheryl, and Grandpa Benjamin had heard the news of the mishap, driven there, and somehow managed to get down to where Brent had fallen and joined the nurse. Their story was remarkable.

When the EMT's had painstakingly hoisted the stretcher to the top with Brent in it, the nurse and her crew looked up to where they had climbed down, and there was no getting back out that way, especially in the night. They had to be rappelled back up one by one, which was not very gentle. Their arms, the front of their bodies, and the sides of their faces were badly scrapped and bruised. They reported that the rescue unit surmised Brent had fallen 60 feet, but that it was the cleanest fall they had attended to that summer compared to others. They also reported that when the paramedics arrived, they threw their huge bag of first- aid medicine down ahead of them, hoping the people below would catch it. However, because it was so heavy, it fell so fast that all they heard was a WHOOSH! Uncle Benjamin started to reach for it, but the nurse grabbed him and pulled him back. It would have simply taken him down with it. Six hundred dollars worth of medication fell six hundred feet into Canyon De Chelly.

Only a four foot ledge that jutted out from the cave-like place where he fell saved his life. This ledge broke his fall, and he buckled to the right into the cave. If he had fallen to the left, he could have toppled over the edge six or seven hundred feet to the canyon floor.

In the emergency room, the doctors saw Brent's left leg was busted below the knee, and it was very swollen. They could not get a pulse in it, so they slit both sides of the leg to relieve the pressure that was building up and preventing blood flow to his feet. A hematoma was forming in his head and there was the possibility of spinal injury. The good sign was that he was able to move his feet and feel in them. Since the Chinle Compehensive Hospital lacks sophisticated equipment to treat such trauma, the decision was made to air lift him out to a trauma unit in Farmington, NM. Again Tara accompanied her brother on the plane.

A CAT scan at the San Juan Regional Medical Center revealed three lower backbones and his right heel were also broken. He was experiencing such excruciating pain in his busted leg. Thus, began two months of painful surgeries on his leg, back and heel. The fall could have been so much worse. He could have fallen head first and busted his head open, and he could have severed his spinal cord and become paralyzed. I still shudder to think about what could have happened. Brent was very, very lucky to walk away from this ordeal.

Shortly after the three successful surgeries on his leg, three lower backbones, and his heel, Brent began experiencing chest pains. The doctors were afraid blood clots may have formed at one of the surgical sites and traveling through his body. They explained to Chei Lee and me that this was common from extensive surgery, and that one could lodge in his heart or brain. "It could be fatal," they said. I could not take it anymore, first the fall, then the surgeries, and now this. I was devastated! "Oh no, how can this happen? Everything seemed to be going well!" I shouted at Chei Lee, as if it was his fault. I reached out to all the religious groups I knew of and beseeched them for prayers, for I felt nothing short of divine intervention or a miracle was needed here.

Uncle/Grandpa Benjamin and his wife, at the time, traveled to the Mescalero reservation for help. They felt by getting in touch with our Mescalero ancestral ways of healing, he would help his nephew. Several years earlier, we had gotten to know a particular Mescalero woman when my brothers, sisters, and I had gone there searching for our roots. She told us how impossible it would be to try to find any relatives, for there were numerous accounts of abductions similar to ours. She told us she would be our sister, our connection to the Mescalero culture. When Benjamin told her of Brent's ordeal, she said she would engage in an all night vigil of prayers that night to the Gahi for her nephew. That same night in his sleep, Brent dreamed:

Out of the darkness they came, bobbing up and down.
I was not sure what they were at first but I was not afraid.
Soon I heard bells on their dresses, jingling.
I did not see the bonfire, but I could tell there was one.
Firelight flickered off the adornment on their arms and dresses.
As they came into view, they were Gahi.
They danced in full regalia before moving out the same way they came.

Today I believe strongly that the Gahi visited my son in his dream as a direct result of my sister's prayers back in Mescalero, New Mexico. She called to them wholeheartedly in the ways of the ancestors to make it happen. Some may call it magic, but to me it was a spiritual intervention. Another MRI the following week revealed no more signs of blood clots in Brent's body. He was on his way to full recovery. After the traumatic ordeal, Brent returned to school and earned a Master's Degree in school counseling from the San Diego State University in California. When he went there to enroll, we accompanied him. While he was registering, we drove to the ocean to place an offering to the big ocean of the west (our grandmother) and to ask it to protect our son while he was going to be away from home.

Like little children they come
Running to parents they haven't seen in so long
Millions of tiny water bubbles, tumbling and dancing
They crowd around the Navajo man's ankle deep in water
He tries to place four horizontal lines of corn pollen on the sandy beach
They would not let him, wanting it all at once
Content, the bubbles rush back into the ocean

When Brent was finished at the university, the whole Naashgali Clan went out to see him graduate with honors. Once more we returned to the ocean, this time to give thanks to it for watching over our son and to bid it farewell for now. I was so grateful that my family would be reunited again back at home on the reservation.

Again we stand on the sandy shore of the Pacific
Waves come but stop short of four yellow lines on the wet sand
Slowly they come, small waves lapping up the lines one by one
We watch and listen to the prayer
One last wave approaches
Large and swift, it covers the last line
And returns to the depth of itself

Brent returned home to work in the Chinle School District, living in his late grandparents' old house.

I am also very happy and thankful for the beautiful young women my daughters have become in their own unique ways. Leigh Ann is K'ehanibaa', my Seeker of Happiness, and Tara is K'eyilnibaa, my Bringer of Happiness. They have brought so much joy into my life. Each one is her own person, but I see in them a lot of myself when I was also an aspiring young woman. I have tried to instill in them the same teachings and values my mother gave me in being a Navajo woman and raising a family.

With the help of Lee's parents and his aunt and my sisters, I sponsored the Puberty Ceremony for both of them.

Ann's grandmothers of Kayenta tied her hair, molded her body, baked the earth cake, and pretty much took care of everything else for her ceremony. Of course her late Grandma Lilly, her dad's aunt was also there to help. Ann's grandparents asked an old man named Red Beard from Many Farms to sing the Hogan song for her.

Leigh Ann has always been my right hand person, usually standing right there next to me whenever we have a big ceremony like a Night Way/ Ye'iibichei, a Fire Dance/ Nahast'ei tl'ee' Na'at'ooyee bika' ji Hataal, or an Enemy Way/ Nidaa' Ceremony. Today, though, I have slowed down significantly, and the situation has reversed itself. Now I try to stand by her while she takes the reins in hand.

She has had her own rough start. At two months, she developed some kind of stomach flu for which she had to be hospitalized. It did not respond to any of the antibiotics treatment she was given and it hung on for weeks. At one point, she became so dehydrated, and her skin color became so dark that the doctors did not expect her to live through the night. Before she went into the hospital, she was a healthy and happy 14 pound baby. That night she was down to 7 lbs, her birth weight. We were distraught! Some relatives of my husband helped us set up a Peyote meeting, and during the night our baby recovered from whatever was making her sick. The doctors and nurses at the Fort Defiance Hospital were surprised and could not explain what happened. She is another reason your Chei Lee and I decided to follow the Peyote Way of praying.

Sometimes Ann accused us of not loving her enough because she is the middle child. She couldn't have been more wrong. We loved her and continue to love her with all our hearts today. She gave us three beautiful grandchildren that make our hearts content and our lives complete.

In high school, Ann developed an interest in the sport of rodeo as a barrel-racer and break- away- roper. She found a cowboy husband who now traveled with her to rodeos, leaving her father free to do other things. Before that it was her father accompanying her to high school and college rodeos. Jacob Antone came from a long line of champions in rodeo events. Later he took World Championship in Steer Wrestling at the INFR in Albuquerque two times in a row.

One winter afternoon we were transporting our Ann and her horse to a rodeo. Shortly out of town, we saw a horse racing at full speed toward us inside the fence running along the highway. We noticed the saddle first and thought it must have run away from its rider. Within that instant, Ann exclaimed, "It's dragging something or someone!" The runaway horse barreled toward us as whatever it was swung from side to side behind it. Instantly, your Chei Lee swung the truck and horse trailer off to the side of the highway, and before the truck came to a full stop Ann was out of the truck and dashing toward the fence. With incredible speed and agility, she was over the six strand barbed-wire fence.

By that time the horse slowed, perhaps startled by Leigh Ann, and it stopped abruptly when she shouted, "Whoa!" She grabbed the reins and held on with all her might, trying to calm it and at the same time by repeating, "shish, shish" to it softly. With nostrils flaring and sides heaving, the runaway horse tried to obey the tiny girl that had managed to stop it, but ready to speed off again at the slightest spook. It was dragging a person, a man as it turned out.

A man driving on that side of the fence and seeing what was happening also stopped his truck and ran as fast as he could toward the horse in spite of Ann's motion to him to stay back. At that instant, the horse reared up again and almost tore the reins from Ann's hands. Her dad who was just coming from the other side of the fence lunged over and grabbed the reins at the mouth piece. The horse calmed once more, and while Ann and her dad held the horse, the other man loosened the rope from around the poor, frightened man's ankle after several failed attempts.

The unfortunate man appeared youngish, in his twenties. Mud covered his entire body and glistened under the late afternoon sun. His clothes had peeled off him somewhere, as he did not have a stitch on. His leg, twisted like a pretzel, seemed badly dislocated from its socket at the hip, and he was in terrible pain.

I have always heard people say an individual will assume incredible courage and strength in an emergency situation that he/she or others never thought possible. Well, I saw it in action that day when 110 pound Leigh Ann stopped a thousand pound of energy hurtling at her.

Leigh Ann has three children. Her oldest is Ashkii Lee. He is sixteen years old and in the eleventh grade. I'm sure he gets his height from his father's side of the family where most of his uncles are tall. Even his naalii man seems tall and lean in the only picture Jacob has of his father. In fact, Ashkii resembles this man more than anybody else. Ashkii plays basketball in high school, but his real talent lies in drumming and singing in peyote ceremonies. He is a very handsome boy, and I'm not just saying that as his grandmother.

Jacob's father was half White which accounts for ten year old Amanda's almost blonde hair. She is the second child. Her skin is so fair that she can pass for a white girl. I gave her the Navajo name, Taosbaa' Chih. Manda is a baseball player. I know she will grow up to be a beautiful girl.

Last but not least, is Stephen Dineh Antone. He is my absolute pride and joy. At four, he is not tall and lean but thick and stocky like his dad. Here is a football player and a future steer wrestler.

Tara Lee came four years after Leigh Ann. She was daddy's girl from the start; in fact, both girls were closer to their dad while Brent was a child after my own heart. We both enjoyed reading and writing. He also enjoyed writing poetry, sketching, and playing his saxophone. When Tara began school, her dad gave her a five dollar bill every day, so there was a joke going about how her dad paid her to go to school.

One summer when Tara was dating Terry, Grandpa Brent took them to Hopi dances over on the Hopi Reservation. As they were walking off after watching a dance, a clown ran after them, caught Terry, and went through the motion of having sex with him. It turned out the clown represened fertility in the dance. After that it was inevitable that soon they would have a baby together.

While Brent and Ann were raised by their naaliis until they were three or four, Tara always stayed with us. They never needed baby sitters or day care. I imagine it is this situation that accounted for why they are more fluent in Navajo than Tara. Tara was very imaginative and always saying something funny as a child. Once she touched her forehead and leaned back saying, "Mom, I think I'm homesick." Another time she suggested we restrange the living room. She also wanted to know where the army was when she heard someone was home from the army. At last, she steered my shopping cart toward where the school supplies of staples and staplers were at the store because she had heard me say at home that morning that I was out of staples, and I needed to go to the store to buy some more. Her daughter, Chubby, was even funnier when she ran into the house shouting, "Mommy! Mommy! I saw an eye with one bug!"

On a chilly Sunday afternoon in March, Tara shyly called me aside to tell me she had started her menses. Immediately, we walked next door to notify grandma and grandpa who set the date the ceremony was to start. The next day, a local matriarch arrived adorned in her finest clothes and jewelry. She spread a buffalo robe and ten Pendleton robes and shawls belonging to the women present, one on top of the other. Then she had Tara sit on the layers of blankets while she brushed her hair with a straw brush and tied it with a buckskin string taken from the skin of an unwounded fawn. (Tara's grandmother happened to have one of this kind and we still have it in the family today). Next she molded and massaged Tara's body as she lay flat on her stomach. After that she instructed her to pull everyone present upward and return the blankets to their owners. Then she was instructed to run out of the hogan with a string of people running after her. She would continue to do so two times a day for the rest of the ceremony. (Other women instruct young girls to run three times a day, but Tara's grandmother advised against it saying negative spirits abound in late evenings, and it's not good to run during that time).

The rest of the week, her grandmothers roasted, ground, and sifted the corn. By Thursday evening we had four sacks of corn meal. Later that evening, two men dug a hole in the ground with the circumference as wide as the length of a shovel and built a fire in it.

The big day dawned crisp and cold. We butchered two one year old lambs. In the afternoon eight women arrived bringing their stirring sticks and mixed the cornmeal with hot boiling water rushed in by men tending the fire. While the batter was cooling a large mutton dinner was served to everyone. Later that evening the medicine man came and bantered with the other men before the night-long ritual. At dawn the matriarch washed Tara's hair in sudsy yucca root, and instructed her to run for the last time. Long icicles hung from her hair as she ran back into the hogan.

Before everyone went home, another large meal was served to all present along with slices of corn cake. The large inner pieces were distributed to the medicine man and the people who sang during the night; the smaller outer ones were given to people who helped throughout the week. At last, the long event ended, and No, I did not have a second kinaalda ceremony for Tara upon her second menses.

At the beginning of her junior year Tara became pregnant, much against what we had always tried to teach her. She was only sixteen and had a very tough go of her pregnancy. Tara developed a condition called pre-eclampsia where her blood pressure soared out of control. She had to be hospitalized and put on bed rest. To avoid any distress on the baby, Tara was flown out to the Good Samaritan Hospital in Phoenix. As a result, Stephanie came two months early by Cecerean.

With Chubby, things were not any different; in fact, they worsened. Again Tara developed pre-eclampsia and had to go into the hospital early. This time, the baby developed a low heart beat that required Tara to be flown out again to the Good Samaritan Hospital, earlier than with Steph.

Your Chei Lee just happened to be visiting her when the decision was made, so he got on the plane with her. Somehow he must have gotten away, while paper work was prepared, to go home and leave me a note. I raced up to the hospital, but the plane had already left. I came home feeling so sad and lonely that I wept as I sat at the table. Why! Why was this happening to my baby?

The next day the rest of us followed. Chubs had been delivered, and we found this tiny little bundle wrapped in a blanket. Everyone took a sign of relief, thinking now that the baby was delivered, Tara was out of the woods. However, that was not to be. Overnight, her body swelled up so much that her eyes were just narrow slits, and she looked like a blimp the next day. All the time people were rejoicing, I had this lump in my chest indicating to me that things were not really okay. Sometimes I get this feeling that I don't like. I seem to know something bad is going to happen before it happens. Sure enough, the doctors told us the condition had taken its toll on Tara's kidneys and liver, and that was the reason for all the swelling. They pointed out to us that if she continued to have any more pregnancies, they would cause these organs to fail.

Tara was in and out of consciousness and could not make any decisions, and Terry had not arrived at the hospital yet. Thus, I took it upon myself to make a major decision for my daughter to have a tubal ligation. Once one of you asked me why I chose to do this when I was so adamant about going against the traditional teachings of our people. I remember telling you that I appreciated any grand babies that would have come but I loved my daughter more. After all, I had watched her grow up and had known her for sixteen years. I did not want to lose her. Later, when she had recovered from the ordeal, she informed me she had already made that decision. It wasn't until we had come home to the reservation and conducted a ceremony that the lump in my chest went away.

For some strange reason, all three of my children had to suffer pain and illness at some point in their lives. As a result, though, they have gone on to become well rounded, strong individuals. You know how they are very active in the community through the traditional ceremonies and through the Chinle school system. Sometimes I wonder if the sincerity of my husband and our belief in the "Medicine" and the way of life we chose to follow was tested by a higher power through what we cherish and love the most, our children.

Chubby suffered from Asthma during her growing up years. The least little contact with horses and hay makes her wheeze and her eyes water. As a result, she couldn't hang out at her Aunt Leigh Ann's house. As you know, the girls grew up and thrived. Tara sponsored the Puberty Ceremony when Stephanie came of age.

Stephanie's first kinalda went very well, except an inch or two of the top of the cake burned. With my sisters, we prepared the cornmeal for the cake very carefully. We roasted the corn to a golden-brown and sifted it well. We used boiling water to mix the meal and stirred the mush to the right consistency. Our batter was golden from the enzymes of the chewed cornmeal and sugar, boiled brown sugar, and raisins as we poured it into the ground.

Some parts around the edge and some in the center were not burned all the way. Those we brushed the ashes and black coals from and sliced off the burnt crust. Thus, we gave thin slices of cake to the six singers and the medicine man, rather than thick, square pieces as usually is the case. Despite the black top, the cake underneath was golden with a firm texture, and it was very tasty. I have tasted puberty cake that has baked nicely, and it has been white and tasteless. Ours was golden, speckled with raisins, and sweet.

Tara was so unhappy that she cried as she spoke to thank us for helping her with the ceremony. "Everything else went so well, and my daughter looked so beautiful. Why did her cake have to burn?" she asked. She blamed herself for just leaving the responsibility of taking care of the fire on Terry and the guys once the cake was put in the ground.

Six big men over saw the fire, and in trying to do the right thing, unknowingly kept adding too much wood to the fire. I had seen the fire earlier and thought to go out and check on it, but it slipped my mind as I got very busy with many other things. Even the medicine man said that indeed there was too much fire at midnight and wanted to say something but didn't.

The rest of the ceremony went fantastically well. We asked a maternal uncle by clan to sing the Hogan Song. Six other men turned out and sang beautiful horse, mountain, journey, and wealth songs. There was a full house with most of the family members present. It was a beautiful ceremony; I had not witnessed one with this many medicine people since I was a little girl.

For the washing of Stephanie's hair at dawn, the water just flowed through the basket because it was so loosely woven. Most baskets are made that way these days! I managed to work up some suds and rub it into her long, thick hair. Due to this, I was done washing her hair in one song.

Usually there are four songs to do it in. When the last song was done, she ran out of the hogan with fifteen or more people trailing after her. The medicine man sang only two of four songs thinking she would be running back right away. He said that was what other girls did that he had sung the Blessing Way for, but he did not know that Stephanie was a runner.

The four day Kinaalda Ceremony ended with a large meal served to all. Paper sacks of cake slices and pieces were also distributed to all. With Steph's second menses and ceremony we vowed to be more careful. Of course that happen in Black Rock, and this time we out did ourselves and everything turned out beautifully.

As you know Tara married into a Pow-wow family. At first she and her family danced and I used to like seeing that thinking, 'The family that dances together, stays together.' After awhile Tara stopped dancing and began concentrating on her girls, making sure they had the proper attire: dresses, shawls, bead work, moccasins, and jewelry. The girls as fancy-shawl dancers began contesting and winning monetary and other awards. Terry continued to dance from time to time, and he and Tara have taken the girls all over the country, even into Canada. Many young girls emulate Stephanie and have often said they wish they can dance like her. Steph has perfected her footwork, and Chubby is getting there. It really is a joy to watch the girls dance as they twirl round and round to the rhythm of the drum and song until the colors become a blur.

LOSING HAROLD

Harold Steven Begay was my oldest sister, Betty's son, but I always thought of him as my own. We lost him one early autumn morning in 2004 when he took his own life. It has been so painful, especially for me, and still is today. Some of my brothers and sisters wonder why I still grieve my son's passing. A man I used to work with who lost an only child, told me then that time does not help make the pain better as people say, and I think he is right. I wish I can take back time and tell Harold again how much I love him and care about him. Harold knew well enough he was loved by all of his aunts, uncles, brothers, sisters, nephews, and nieces. That is not what bothers me today. It's that he was all alone when he must have grappled with the decision to end his life. The rest of the family was at the Window Rock Fair. Not one of us had offered to invite him to go with us! I will be haunted by this realization for the rest of my life. I feel we failed mother who instructed us to look after one another and our children.

It wasn't that we had not seen enough signs from him; on a couple occasions family members saw a noose hanging from the roof top and from the arbor. We ignored it thinking he didn't mean anything by it, he was just fooling around. You see, Harold got into drugs and alcohol early in his life. We did what we could to help him by sending him to rehab, sponsoring traditional ceremonies, and just talking to him. They did not seem to really help. He stayed clean and sober for a couple of months, and he was back into them again.

Another reaction I felt over Harold's passing was that of anger at the deities especially mother earth and father sky for taking him and being so impartial and indifferent. The days were continuing as if nothing out of the ordinary had happened. I don't know if a mere person has a right to express anger at the holy people. Deep down, though, I feel they took him back unto themselves because they saw how lonely and dejected he felt here on earth. Did Harold choose a time when no one was around to carry out what he had been planning for some time? There was no family around, just a feeling of hopelessness with no way out of how and what he was feeling that day. Oh God, how could we have been so selfish?

We all know Harold put a noose around his neck and hanged himself. The thing that I still wonder about also is how the police found numerous scratch marks on a limb next to where he was hanging. It's almost like he had a change of heart at the last minute and tried to grab for it. That's what I want to believe. I don't know, though, and we'll probably never know.

We all stayed in Black Rock to observe the four days after the burial of a family member. On the second day, rain began shortly before midnight. It rained the rest of the night, all morning, and part of the next day. The footsteps of our dear son on his painful journey on earth were being washed away, (bikek'eehoolta). His passing from this life was blessed with the sacred rain. He was brought into this world with to'alanashchiin and tobiyaazh, and he left it in the same way. Our son who was not a man of knowledge and power was blessed by the holy people that took pity on him and came down in throng and sound to take him back unto themselves. Our elders often say only powerful medicine men are blessed this way in their passing. We will take this event to heart and find strength and comfort as we go on in life without Harold. We will know he is near when we hear the rumble of thunder and smell the earthy scent of rain close by.

I am not a poet in any sense of the word but I created this during the time Harold went away as I was trying to cope with his passing:

What Happens to Us?

On a great celestial road, a host of people travel

Throngs of men, women, and children move with packs on their backs

Their time on earth is over, and they have to be here

They have a common destination

There is much commotion and din: laughter and singing

This is replaced by thunder rumbles, thunder crashes, lightning flashes

When people die, they return to nature

They go to live with the holy people

Thunder is their voice

Lightning is their light to guide them
They return to earth as rain, snow, sleet, and hail
They become the waters of the earth
Sometimes in their travels, they may come upon a familiar face
They must not stop to communicate, for they no longer can
They must continue their journey, returning again and again for all
eternity

An unusual phenomenon occurred a month after we put Harold into the ground. Ashikii started having recurring dreams. It was always about Harold walking down the hill from where he was buried. He would come to his mother's brush arbor and begin looking for something as he lifted stuff and looked under them. Then he would go into the house and do the same thing. At last he looked under his old bike sitting behind his mother's house. At one point Ashkii said he asked Harold what he was looking for, but Harold ignored him and kept searching. Shortly, Ashkii became withdrawn and his school work began to suffer.

One day Ann asked her father to pray for him. His grandfather asked Ashkii to bring his instrument box he carries to peyote meetings. As Ashkii opened his box, his grandfather saw right on top lay a feather fan that belonged to Harold. Lee remembered Victoria had given it to him months earlier for safe-keeping. He said she was afraid at the time that Harold would sell it or put it in pawn, and it would become lost. Ashkii must have picked it up and put it in his box without telling his grandpa about it. That was the root of Ashkii's problem. Once it was revealed, the dreams stopped, and Ashkii got better.

CARING FOR
THE SHEEP

Today I stay home and care for my sheep that Chei Lee's grandparents left us. In Lee's family, ownership of the land has been carried on by the male offspring for many years. This as you know is contrary to the common belief and practice of a man going to live with his wife's people. They are the only Navajo family that I know of that practices patriarchal ways. Years ago, his father went to Kayenta and brought his new bride to live with him on his land. When my husband and I married, he took me to live with him here. With the passing of his father, he took the responsibility of taking care of the land, the grazing permit, the land use permit, and the home site lease. As it is, Brent is next in line to maintain the land base. In this way, it seems, ownership of the land goes to a different clan.

When the old folks got too old to care for the herd anymore, they had the grazing permit divided between Chei Lee and his uncle Kee. Much earlier, My mother had separated a few heads from her own herd when your Chei Lee and I were married to bring with me into my marriage. I like to think their blood line continues in the herd that we have today. While I was working, I neglected the herd full time. As a result, we lost many lambs every spring. To care for the sheep was the number one reason I chose to retire early from my job.

Many lambs came on cold winter nights and froze when Lee and I became their caretakers. I remember my parents and Chei Lee's parents getting up in the middle of the night and bringing new born lambs inside their homes. Sometimes they had two ewes standing with their lambs inside their one room dwellings. I have never brought sheep into my home, but we do make sure the corral is covered securely to keep out the cold wind. One day, all the sheep decided to drop their lambs at one time. Some had twins and others single ones. When Chei Lee and I returned home, we did not know which lamb belonged to which ewe. We just saw lambs crawling everywhere trying to find their mothers. As a result, we lost eight lambs that evening.

I also look after the cornfield. While I was working, the corn would ripen just as I was returning to work in the fall. Thus, I did not make use of the freshly ripen corn, and they just became over-ripe, dry, and hard. I managed to make some kneel-down bread, charred ears of corn, and more kneel-down bread to dry out for winter. Eventually, with the help of my children and Chei Lee, we steamed some.The majority of it, we left to dry out.

The summer I went to Hawaii, I grew award winning corn. The cornstalk grew about fourteen or fifteen feet tall. I don't know how that happened, but Brent had bought the corn seed at the Gallup Flea Market that spring. I decided to enter the stalks at the Navajo Tribal Fair in Window Rock. I had Chei Lee dig one up and I transported it to the fair. When I went into the agriculture building, I saw all these tall corn stalks leaning against a table and my heart sank. They all seemed so much taller than mine. What was I thinking? However, I had driven seventy miles in a down pour, and there was no turning back. A guy helped me unload my corn stalk and stood it next to the others that were already there. By far, my cornstalk towered higher than all of them. "What did you do to grow the biggest and tallest corn?" the officials asked. "Nothing", I said. My husband and I planted it and I left for Hawaii. When I returned, that is what I found." Anyway, my cornstalk took the blue ribbon for first place that time.

A MAN CAME
THROUGH OUR LIVES

The summer I retired from Dine College, your Chei Lee began building a house, a log cabin to be exact. Many people came to help when they weren't working and were free to do so. Your uncle Garrick was instrumental from the beginning with the laying of the foundation, the floor, and the stacking and fitting of the logs. A man that was most instrumental in the building of the house was someone whom we had met five or six years earlier. He called us one day and asked us to conduct a Peyote meeting for the executive officers of the Azee' Beenahagha of Dine Nation, the new name for the Native American Church of Navajoland. He was part of this organization and responsible for taking care of details, and he wanted the meeting done in Mirando City, TX.

Every April, the officers of the organization and members return to the "Peyote Garden," in southern Texas, the only place peyote grows in this country. They conduct ceremonies there in memory of the ancestors and elders who have paved the way for them. They travel south on the 285 highway from Clines Corner and call it the ancient road (atiin sani). In the ceremonies there, they talk about the first couple that went there to obtain medicine and pray that today's Navajo children can continue the tradition and never lose sight of it. They also reminisce about the time a young man put himself on the line on purpose, by getting arrested for carrying peyote illegally out of Texas. See, before that it was illegal to transport peyote. Even here on the reservation, the tribal government forbade its use. This young man risked going to jail just so peyote could be legalized and his people could use it in ceremonies. The event that happens in the spring is called, The Pilgrimage.

Most of you don't know the origin of this organization though you and your families have meetings and partake of peyote. With 'Church' in the former name, white people did not hesitate to begin partaking of the medicine and even conducting prayer services, citing freedom of religion. Our leaders suggested this was the only ceremony we have left and did not want to share it with these foreigners. They had intruded into everything else. The name took back the literal and traditional meaning of how our elders referred to the plant that we eat during a peyote meeting to ask for physical, mental, emotional, and spiritual strength. To us it is a medicine (azee'). In the early days 'Church" was included in the name because it was the only way the US Government would allow the Native Americans to use it for ceremonial purposes. The peyote ceremony has a long history.

Anyway, we have gone back to Texas on the pilgrimage many times after that to pray for the leaders of the organization and other times we just go for ourselves. The man that came to ask us to conduct a ceremony for the organization for the first time began coming around to our house after that. He and Chei Lee just seem to click from the start. They turned out to be brothers by clans and just became inseparable. He began following us and helping us conduct our peyote ceremonies back here on the reservation. In fact he would go ahead of us to a meeting place and have the fire going and be sitting at the fire chief's position ready to go when we finally got there.

This man was my paternal grandfather according to clan, my naalii. He was a carpenter by trade and began driving from Tuba City to help his brother build the cabin. He never asked for any pay. Soon he began bringing his sons who had learned the trade from him to help him. Sometimes they spent the night, and I always made sure they had plenty of food to eat which of course didn't make up for the work they did. One time my naalii heard me say I saw how expensive cabinets were. He said for me not to worry about buying cabinets and that he would build them. He made me laugh when he added that white people were not the only ones that can build cabinets that he could too.

Alas, my wonderful naalii died the following spring at age fifty-eight on Mother's Day, leaving his wife, children, and grandchildren. Chei Lee was devastated. He didn't work on the house the rest of the summer or fall. My naalii was such a jolly man, always joking and laughing, and that was what they did those times when they worked on the house. Everything about the construction of the cabin just came to a standstill, until January 2009. Then Chei Lee went back out and slowly began working again. Soon a crew of brothers came and began putting in the drywall, and the sons of my naalii came back and finished some of the outside work. Then we paid a man out of Cortez to wash the logs down on the outside and apply a protective, shiny cover to it.

STORIES ARISING FROM WRITING ASSIGNMENTS

There are some memories that I want to share with you before I close my story. They and all the others I have so far told you grew out of writing assignments I had my classes do at Dine College. Whenever, I assigned anything, I often found that I also had a similar experience. I believe that is why I enjoyed teaching writing because I could write right along with the students.

There is a very funny moment I want to share with you. Once I took my friend's jacket home by mistake, and she took mine. I had just started working in the English Department in the fall of 1982. Although it was late fall, the sky was clear blue and the day was warm. Suddenly I noticed the time and realized the Transit Bus was almost there. Quickly, I grabbed my maroon leather jacket from the rack where my friend Delilah also hung her maroon jacket and raced to the Bus Stop where it was getting ready to pull out.

The next day I rode the bus to work again. Because it is colder in Tsaile than Chinle, I put my jacket on when I got off the bus. Immediately, I realize it was larger than usual. When I drew the front together, they crossed over all the way to my underarm. Surprised, I wondered how I could have suddenly lost so much weight. At that point, what must have happened the day before dawned on me. I had run off with Delilah's jacket! It was so hilarious that I laughed all the way to the office. When I got to the office, there sat my friend, laughing. She's a tall, husky woman, and when she tried to get my jacket on that morning, she said she couldn't get it over her shoulders. She also wondered how she had suddenly gained so

87

much weight overnight. We had a good laugh about the incident, with tears running down our faces.

Another time, I asked the class to write about an embarrassing moment. I wrote about the time I misplaced my truck keys in a most inconspicuous place. Spring semester had ended for me at NAU where I was finishing up graduate school in 1984. I was driving the children back for their last week in the Flagstaff school system. They were very excited about spring and the last week of school, and some of that excitement was rubbing off on me. Little did I know that very soon I would misplace my truck keys, and I would be very embarrassed to find them in a most unlikely place. I would look high and low and everywhere before I found them.

After the kids ran into the school building, I drove to the Big Boy Restaurant across from the university. Since I had been driving all morning, I went into the bathroom to freshen up. Then I sat at a small table by a window overlooking the city of Flagstaff. As I ate my breakfast, I wondered about what I would do with myself that day and the rest of the week.

When I finished my breakfast, I walked to my truck. I opened my purse to take out the keys, but they weren't there. Surprised, I looked inside the truck through the window to see if I didn't leave them in the ignition. When I did not see them there, I emptied my purse on the ground but still no keys.

I ran back into the restaurant to see if the waitress found them and even went back to the restroom to look. The keys were nowhere to be found. Within minutes, the whole restaurant staff was searching the premise with me, and I was beginning to panic. I just couldn't imagine what could have happened to the large set of keys on a leather boot key ring. They just seem to have vanished.

Two service attendants eating in the restaurant tried to help. They said to come over to their station if the keys did not turn up and they would call a locksmith to make a duplicate key for the truck. "It'll cost you, though," one of them said. I suddenly felt very frightened and lonely. Close to tears I ran back to the restroom. As I pulled my pants down, the keys fell to the floor. They were inside my pants all the time! However, I couldn't understand how I wasn't able to feel its bulk against my body. Because I was too ashamed to tell anyone about my discovery, I walked slowly out of the restaurant, walked to my truck, and drove away. The restaurant staff probably continued to search.

This incident did not deter us from having a good time, going to the mall, shopping, and watching movies the rest of the week. Only later when enough time had passed was I able to tell my family about the incident. And only then was I able to laugh about it. Now when I think back to what happened, I can't help but laugh at my stupidity.

SPONSORING
CEREMONIES

My sisters, brothers, and I have sponsored our share of large ceremonies, one of them being the Enemy Way Ceremony or "Squaw Dance". This is a summer, healing ceremony involving not just the family but the whole clan. It is expensive, requiring lots of money and sheep. Usually the community comes out and donates items needed, but the large bulk comes from the family. Usually a family has strong means to carry out one of these ceremonies. People are working and have money to secure the necessary items and a sheep herd which is most important to feed the many people that will come.

With the guidance and help of your Chei Lee and his family we were able to do a nine night Night Way or Ye'iibichei Ceremony and three Enemy Way. My mother and her family did not have the means to pull off a big ceremony like these. There were also no elders with strong knowledge of the sacred stories to speak for us. Mother could only co-sponsor one, meaning when a family was sponsoring a big ceremony, she could ask if a sick relative could be part of the ceremony.

The first Enemy Way was for Brent. As a child, he had carried out the duty of a Sits Between for his paternal grandparents whenever his grandfather was having a Nidaa'. As, such he could then receive the ceremonial staff with guidance from his grandfather. Once he had received the staff again when the drum just melted from the water inside it. This meant the clay pottery had not been fired before we bought it. We already had a pottery or drum carried on by the grandfather for many years, but we wanted to use a newer, shiny one this time. Thus, you can see, newer is not always better. The ceremony had to be stopped, for something like this was not supposed to happen. Chei Lee and I went away knowing that now we had our work cut out for us. We had to sponsor a Nidaa' from scratch for our son the following summer to repair or fix the mishap.

Then Chei Lee and Brent received the ceremonial staff several times, and my sisters and I cooked and fed the party of the main sponsors and the people that came. That is no small task, but we always managed to pull them off.

The second Enemy Way was for Tara upon Brent's suggestion. See, several years earlier, Chei Lee had received the staff from Many Farms. After all the goods were thrown out, bundles given to perspective recipients, and the people left, Tara was deeply affected by the spirit of the ceremony. She became very lethargic, confused, and broke out in a sweat. This ceremony, like any other ceremony, is so powerful and not to be taken lightly as the name suggests, "Squaw Dance". If care is not taken, it can affect someone, (diitl'i'). Immediately, her dad picked her up and took her to the home of a man for him to "restore" her. He is a practitioner of the Enemy Way Ceremony. Only people like him who know songs and prayers of this nature are able to restore people. This is true of every other ceremony. Tara came home smiling and being her old self. Brent said this ritual was like just putting a band aid on a wound that she will probably feel better for a while, but it would come back to affect her again. Therefore, he suggested we sponsor the whole ceremony for her to get fully well.

The following summer we sponsored the ceremony. A local youngster relative of Chei Lee served as the "Sits Between" for Tara and Ashkii whose function was to carry the staff for Tara and kill the bad spirit affecting Tara, on the last day. At the "First Night" there was dancing. My granddaughters dressed up in their Mescalero Apache camp dresses their Uncle Brent bought for them. They looked so elegant and beautiful as they danced round and round with different partners. Of course, as their mother took them around to ask prospective young men to dance, she had to ask them what their clans are. If they were not of the same clan the girls were, the girls pulled them out to dance. Some came willingly while others resisted, but they came eventually. The girls liked dancing with the older gentlemen, though, because they said these guys paid more.

Saturday back at the main camp, things began jumping as soon as we got back. A couple had already brought a goat and a man, groceries. It was nonstop after that. People flowed in like water from both entrances into the food arbor with loads of groceries. My brother Fred led some men to begin butchering again, and we fed people right and left. Everyone asked for ribs, but a sheep has only two ribs! Though women fileted meat like crazy, it was never enough. This went on all day and evening, slowing down only until dusk. So many people came from far and near to help my daughter. No one came into the arbor empty handed. While my sisters and I and our clan relatives busied ourselves at the food arbor, Brent and Chei Lee with the help of other men also busied themselves with gathering and preparing herbs for the ceremony at the hogan.

Many women and girls made tons of frybread and ashbread in the cooking area under the hot blazing sun. Bless their hearts; they wiped away sweat and worked nonstop. We kept them supplied with cold sodas and water. Inside the arbor, air conditioners and swamp coolers were running full speed while people enjoyed feasting on mutton. You'd think they had never seen mutton before. It was a wonderful exchange, though; they gave and we returned. That's the way the Navajo people are. The relatives and community are the ones that make a large ceremony possible.

No sooner had the day's activities slowed down, then; it was time to prepare for the next day. My sisters and nieces cut up tons of potatoes for the breakfast we would serve the First Night party. Tomorrow would be a big day, for the First Night people would be arriving in full force. Two big meals had to be served, goodies tossed out, and valuables exchanged. Shortly after sun up, horse backs from both camps met, shouting: "Eh, Eh, Eh!" Someone fired a rifle into the air four times as the riders raced around the hogan.

At ch'i'iil kaad or tossing out of goodies, we threw out so many stuff to the party that we bogged them down. They stood in their places unable to move. The women were also burdened with an assortment of cloth goods. Usually people only give stuff to the sponsors; we gave it away to the whole communities of Chinle Valley and Many Farms, it seemed. Everyone will eat Cracker Jack and Popcorn Balls for the next two years.

What an undertaking we carried out. I had to hand it to my children, Brent and Leigh Ann, my husband, and my brothers and sisters. After the large noon feeding, we took a huge sigh of relief. Weedaa exclaimed loudly, "We did it; we pulled it off!"

After Brent, Ann, and Tara there is no foreseeable future for undertakings like this continuing. One has to have grown up hearing the stories, been part of ceremonies, and have spoken the Dine language to do so. I am sorry that many of you have chosen the life of living in cities where the jobs are, but you also have no idea what you have lost out on. Maybe there is hope for your children; maybe one day they will want to return to the reservation.

FAMILY ANIMALS

My story will not be complete without mention of family animals. Navajo families have pets, but not in the sense that white people have them. They are usually just there. As a result I will tell stories about a few of the animals that came to our household and into our lives over the years. Navajo elders teach every family should have a (daadinilei) or dog as protector at the door.

The first dog I want to mention is King, a Collie pup. A man working with your Chei Lee at a construction site in Phoenix gave it to him. As it grew bigger, it became harder to keep him inside the fence when we lived in Phoenix. He was always escaping and the dog pound was forever calling us to pick him up. Thus, we brought him home to the reservation where he had the wide open space to run around. He grew into a large, beautiful dog just like Lassie. He became paralyzed after some careless individual backed into him in a car. We had to have him put down.

Another one is Taffer. She was part German sheperd and part Collie. Again someone at the construction site gave it to Lee, to replace King. Her body assumed German shepherd characteristics with short, smooth hair. Also, her straight pointed ears and her long slender legs were every bit German shepherd. Her color, however, indicated her Collie parentage. Her beautiful golden body was like aspen leaves in late autumn, and she had a wide white collar and white paws. What was striking about Taffer was the human-like qualities she possessed; the very gracefulness with which she moved reminded me of a poised young lady in motion.

Taffer never seemed to let her guard down but would assum a lady like poise even at her worse. Unlike most dogs that take on untidy appearances when they are hungry or ill, Taffer's ears did not fall or flop, her coat did not become dirty and messy, and her tail did not fall between her legs in the presence of a strange dog. Her ears were always erect and pointed. She also did not just throw herself down in a clumsy position but would recline gracefully on her side with her forelegs extended out in front of her and her head held high.

This mix breed was also quite conscious of her eating habits very much like a lady. While other dogs scrambled to wolf their food down all at once, Taffer daintily picked at her food, making sure not a tiny morsel fell to the ground. As a result, the other dogs seemed to sense that Taffer was different and afforded her a degree of respect. They tore food from one another but knew enough to leave Taffer alone. Only until Taffer's appetite had been fully satisfied and she had moved away did they scurry over to lick her dish clean.

Taffer was also very fond of babysitting the sheep dog's litter when the mother was out with the sheep all day. One afternoon, when the sheep had foraged too far across the wash, a flash flood occurred from heavy rains in the mountains. As a result, the sheep dog was unable to bring the sheep back across the wash to the corral that evening. The hungry pups scrambled out of their lean-to shelter waiting for their mother to come. They ran here and there, yelping and whimpering. After a while, Taffer rose from where she was dozing and strolled over to investigate what all the commotion was about. After gently taking each pup by the back of the neck and carrying it back to the shelter, Taffer lay down and tried to comfort them. When the sheep dog was able to swim across the raging wash and come back to feed her litter, she seemed surprised to find Taffer grooming her pups as they curled up sleeping. Taffer knew she had to leave, but from there on she took on the responsibility of looking after the sheep dog's pups.

Yet another canine friend was Boomer. He was a mixed Rothwiler and Mutt that I nursed through a terrible case of Mange the first spring and summer he was with us. He also came to us as a pup, and we adopted him. Ordinarily we don't take strays in, but this one was so cute with six toes on his hind feet, huge paws, and a wide chest even as a pup. Soon he and Rocko, another stray pup that my grand children took in, were following me on my daily walks.

One day both got some kind of disease that made them scratch themselves something terrible. Boomer scratched and scratched until large patches of hair came off his skin and left bald spots. None of the home remedies I applied and what the Vet clinic gave me worked. The doctor said they had what is called Mange. It wasn't until I had them dipped in a large tub of chemicals and medicines that they stopped scratching.

Throughout the summer, Boomer grew bigger, and his mangy coat became slick and glossy. He grew into a huge beautiful dog. Sometimes I became angry with him, especially when he raided the cat food in the tree. He had gotten so long that he simply stood on his hind legs, reached for it, knocked it down, and wolfed it. He slept under the steps of our porch where people saw him and were intimidated by him. The funny thing about Boomer was that he was the biggest wimp of all. He didn't growl at people nor run wild. When I walked with them, he lumbered at my side unlike Rocko who ran about exploring the wash and the cluster of trees bordering the Chinle Wash. In the evening when I arrived home from work, I often tossed him a half eaten sandwich from lunch. He always waited for that treat. One day he didn't appear at the side of the truck, and I wondered where he was.

His biggest fault was running after moving vehicles with Rocko, who incited him. We expected that one day he would run in front of a moving car and get run over if he did not stop it. That's exactly what happened. He ran after my daughter, fell under the left tire, and she ran over him in her jeep. However, she said Boomer immediately ran out from under and ran to the hay barn. That's where Ashkii found him. I think he bled to death from extensive injuries. Poor, poor Boomer; he always looked so sad and doleful. Jacob took the body to the wash and left it under a tree. He was the first dog I cried about.

One last dog worth mentioning is Fossy for Frosty. He was part of a litter left under someone's porch by its mother. We took it and left it at the sheep corral hoping to make it a sheep dog. Usually I brought it inside the hogan in the evening after I fed it bread pieces in milk and broth. One evening I forgot all about the little puppy and went to a fire dance with my children. When we came back later in the night, I did not even think of it and just went to sleep. The next morning, the weather was very cold with frost covering everything. I suddenly remembered the puppy and took it some warm milk and pieces of bread. Lo and behold, there lay the carcass of the puppy. It had frozen stiff! I tried moving it around, but there was no life in him. I just picked it up and tossed it where the sun was shining. The rest of the day I kicked myself thinking about how I could have done this to a helpless little pup.

In the evening after your Chei Lee came home from a meeting, I told him what had happened. On some impulse, I asked him to go to the sheep corral with me. In the back of my mind I was recalling what Aunt Susie had once told us. She said she and Pa found the frozen carcass of a baby goat in Black Rock one winter morning. She said they picked it up and tossed the stiff carcass on top of the roof of the corral. Later in the afternoon while Pa was feeding the sheep, he found the baby goat had come back to life. Lo and behold, as we shone our flashlight into the corral, we saw this tiny furry thing run across the corral. The puppy had thawed out in the sun and come back to life, too. I grabbed it, put it under my coat and carried it back to the house. I found a big box, lined it with newspaper, and put it there. It was so tiny that it fit in the palm of Lee's hand. I was so bewildered and happy at the same time. I named the pup Frosty.

Frosty was a Navajo Mutt, but when I took him for shots at the Vet's, the doctor called him a Border collie. I thought, WOW, he's of an important lineage. He lived with us for three years, until he discovered female dogs in heat. One day he went in search of another one and never returned.

CLOSE CALL

Speaking of Canines, once I had a close call with a couple of them. I had taken a different direction for my daily two mile walk, mainly to check on the whereabouts of my sheep. I walked northward along the bank of the Chinle Wash, carrying a long, thick broom handle that I often carried. I was alert and aware of my surroundings, looking all around me from time to time. With everyone from the community out in Gallup,NM, or at an Enemy Way Ceremony somewhere, the place was very quiet. Even the noisy crows were not raising a raucous this day, as they usually did. No vehicles passed on the road, and no dogs barked.

Suddenly, without warning, two dogs charged at me from out of nowhere, barking, snarling, and growling. I thought for sure they were going to attack me. A cold, pin-prickly chill enveloped me from head to toe. They came within inches of me as I swung back and forth and poked at them with my stick, yelling, "GO!" "GO ON!" the whole time. I took a quick look around, and my heart sank. I was in the middle of a clearing with only my stick between me and the dogs. At that moment, I actually thought I was going to die, attacked and mauled by two vicious Doberman. I was TERRIFIED, for I had seen and heard of enough dog attacks on TV to know that this was possible.

A Russian Oak tree stood a few yards behind me. If I could just get to it, I might survive. However, I also knew I would not get very far before they jumped me. One dog especially, kept coming closer every time, ignoring my stick. The whole time I was stepping backward, inch by inch.

After what seemed like hours, one of the dogs backed off, and the other one followed suit. In the meantime, I continued swinging my stick back and forth and yelling at them. The dogs continued to bark, but they stayed their ground. As soon as I went behind some greasewood bushes, I began walking faster. I wanted to run, but I did not want to incite them again. A few yards more, and I was making a mad dash for home. I had never been so frightened for myself in all my life. I wanted Terry to grab his hunting rifle and shoot them on the spot.

However, as I was running home, I saw his black van race away from home. At home, your Chei Lee said one of the kids had stepped on a rusty nail, and he had rushed her to the emergency room. Lee went back with me, but by the time we got to the site, the dogs had returned inside the fence and were sitting on the steps of the tiny hogan just as innocently as they pleased. A call to the police department earlier had indicated we could not shoot the dogs once they were back inside their enclosed area, and Lee complied with their request, but I know Terry would have shot the dogs if he had been there. My daughter said, "Those kinds of dogs are meant to attack and not back off! How in the world did you get away from them?" I told her I believed the stick I carried saved me.

I was also very afraid, now, for my grandson who often walked that way to get the sheep by himself. His first instinct would be to run from the dogs, inviting chase. The owner said he would get rid of the dogs, but he never did. I just know there should be a law against bringing attack dogs onto the reservation.

Some other animals we own that are worth mentioning in addition to the sheep are a donkey and a Paint horse. There are traditional stories attached to these particular kinds of animals, and it is important to know them.

Story says that in the beginning, the Holy People set about creating various animals of earth. When they were finished, they covered their creation. The debri or leftover items were carried outside and discarded on top of the ash pile. When one of the holy people went outside, he saw something gray with long ears and face trying to stand up on the ash pile. Everyone went outside and saw the thing opening its mouth wide but no sound came forth. Someone grabbed a long reed and stuck it in its mouth, and out erupted a sound only a donkey makes today. Then the holy people took the cover off the new life form they had created and told donkey to lead them. He took off and all the animals followed him around the horizon of the earth. After that it was decreed he would be the leader of life (iina bitsesilei). People say animal owners should own a donkey.

We also have a Paint or Pinto. It is female and her name is Day Break Star. Elders also say it is good to have one of these horses around your home. A sacred story pertains heavily to them, and they are considered very special. They symbolize clarity of mind and balance of life.

In the early days, Changing Woman was sent to live in the western ocean accompanied by holy people. They were driving a herd of Paint horses. One day the horses became listless, so a Blessing Way Ceremony was held for them. However, they tore down the brush enclosure and escaped into the night. Two young men sent after them were unable to turn them around. They must have returned to their home within the four sacred mountains, it was ascertained.

On their way, they left certain marks or signs on the land indicating these Paint came this way. There is a place where many hoof prints of horses are visible (Lii' tse'alkaa' nabitiin). As they raced over Narbona Pass, we see the beginning of what we know as Whiskey Creek today. They are said to have stopped here and urinated. The story is beautiful and continues, but you have to see Chei Lee one winter night to find out the outcome of the story.

On April 9, 2009, Chubby/Alison got her first menses, so we had to put everything on hold to carry out a Kinaalda for her. The ceremony went well, and like her sister before her, lots of great singers came out to sing sacred songs for her. Brent and I were two of the singers. Alas, the cake did not cook very well, though. Only half of it on the southwest side of the hole in the ground was firm enough to hand out to the medicine man and the singers.

We mixed five bags of flour and put in a hole that was too small. We should have used only three or four bags. There was also not enough heat on the floor of the pit, for a crust did not even form at the bottom. We plan to have her second Kinaalda at Black Rock and hope to do better this time. However, the cake still did not bake well though everything else went accordingly. Again, many theories arose: the batter was too watery, the fire was not maintained properly so the ground did not get hot enough, and dancers who dance in the Fire Dance or the Nine Night Male Shooting Way tended the fire, and even the Kinaalda is a dancer. However, Chubby to date has run farthest of all kinaalda in the family. At some time, we have to get it right. Virginia's is not far away. Maybe her cakes/alkaad will be the charm, and they were.

Speaking of my children's and grandchildren's puberty ceremonies reminds me of my own when I was 11 years old. I remember crying my head off not knowing what was happening to me. Grandpa, Son of the Late Wide Man, didn't help matters any by scolding me about it as if I had brought my first menses upon myself.

See, my baby brother Benjamin had taken ill with the hard measles and he was burning up with fever in the middle of summer. Mother and I were taken with him from the Chinle clinic to the Ganado hospital where he was admitted and I stayed at a community house where families of sick patients stayed. This is where it happened and mother knew enough to take me to the hospital and asked some nurses to take care of me.

While we were still at the hospital grandpa rushed to his daughter's side to see what the problem was. When she told him about my condition, he got angry with me for making matters worse for his precious daughter. "What with a sick baby, now she has to attend to starting a puberty ceremony for you," he said. Mother didn't mind though; she was happy for me.

I, too, had a beautiful ceremony at my grandfather's wife's homestead. Rain poured on the day we were putting the cake in the ground. The last day I ran at dawn, the road was so muddy I kept slipping and sliding. An uncle, who was a young man then, ran by me and pulled me up from time to time. Most of the men and women from that time are gone now.

CONCLUSION

At some point, I'm going to have to conclude my story though it just wants to go on and on. It has been quite interesting to go back into the past and re-experience that part of my life. Some experiences would rather remain there, but I brought them out for you guys so you can learn from them, like the pain and shame at the hands of some evil people. We are descendants of that brave Mescalero Woman taken from her home and family and brought here that long ago time. I always told you we are not from a prestigious, wealthy Navajo family but from a captive woman. Because we have such a humble beginning, we should never feel superior to other people just because we get an education, have more money than they do, and own more materialistic things. We are who we are and where we are because of her. Without Mescalero Woman, we would not be anything at all.

If you have not gleaned from my story so far the sort of woman I am/was, let me enlighten you. I want to tell you about my physical, social, emotional, psychological, and moral self. In other words, 'what makes me tick'. Of course you have already seen my spiritual side.

You know I am/was the shortest of all my sisters, standing only 5'0". My Anglo friends always told me I am/was too short for a Navajo, but as you know not all Navajos are tall. I am/was a bit on the plump side like my mother as were all her brothers and sister. Even my father was not very tall. Likewise, I was told that I am/was too fair-skinned to be Indian.

As you know, I come from a large family of four men and six women. I am the second eldest, but many times I have had to assume the elder sister role because Grandma Betty has always had problems with her health. Our dad remarried after mom died and lived with his new family for many years until our stepmother died one year ago, after twenty years. Within this tightly knit family, my siblings and their families look to Chei Lee and me for major decisions and advice. Outside my immediate and extended family, I tend to keep to myself, being very shy and uncomfortable with strangers.

Certain things make me happy, sad, and angry. I am happy when a family member is recognized and honored for an achievement. In the classroom, when I was able to reach a student and was instrumental in some small way in his/her learning process, I was happy. A cowboy mistreating a horse at a rodeo just because he did not place in an event makes me angry. Seeing people get jobs and opportunites based on who they know and not what they know is so maddening.

The behavior that I assume is derived from the informal education my mother gave me. I am not outspoken, for she taught me to observe quietly and to take to heart what the learned had to say. "When one is constantly interrupting, one does not acquire a clear, strong mind." Also, she indicated that I live my own life and not try to be someone I am not. Therefore, when I set my mind on doing something, the action must be meaningful and productive, or I don't do it at all.

At last, many beliefs guide my life, but I will mention only a few. I believe friendship should be long lasting with much give and take attitudes from all the people involved. Trustworthiness is another trait that I admire. A true friend must be willing to carry within a most intimate thought confided to him/her by a friend. Moreover, I believe strongly that marriage is a sacred institution, and that a man should always remain with the wife of his youth and vise-versa. Finally, as you have seen I totally prescribe to and adhere to the ancient practices of our people, for it is in them that lay our hopes and our dreams. I believe people come out of harmony with nature and have to be restored to happiness through a series of chants, rituals and ceremonies. Without the ceremonies as the backbone of our Navajo nation, there will be no more history and no more greatness.

Thus, I am who I am because of parental influence and because I choose to live life sensitively, finding in everything around me a lesson to be learned. I am certain there is no one in the world like me.

The story wants to continue full speed ahead, for there is so much still to be told and will need to be told in the future. I will leave it to one of you to take pen in hand or lap top in lap and continue the story. After all, a story is non ending, meant to be told from one generation to the next. At last, I want to say you are all familiar with Martin Luther King, the black man who had a dream for his people. In the same way, I have a dream for you and I want to leave it with you:

I Have a Dream

I have a dream for my grandchildren
They will remember to come together
They will remember to look after one another
They will remember to respect one another
I have a dream for my grandchildren
They will remember Dine language
They will remember Dine teaching
They will remember Dine values and customs
I have a dream for my grandchildren
They will remember what to do in an illness
They will remember how to do a Kinaalda
They will remember how to plan a Blessing Way
I have a dream for my grandchildren
They will remember their four clans
They will remember who is a relative
They will remember their obligation to clan
I have a dream for my grandchildren
They will remember their humble beginning
They will remember their captive grandmother
They will remember she is their ketl'ool
I have a dream for my grandchildren
They will remember grandma's home
They will remember grandma's fireplace
They will remember grandma's holy water
I have a dream for my grandchildren
They will remember the sacred bundles
They will remember the sacred "medicine"
They will remember grandpa's peyote fireplace
I have a dream for my grandchildren
They will not wander the streets of some city
They will not be ashamed to be called Dine
They will not be overcome by the foreigners
I have a dream for my grandchildren

PHOTOS

My grandfather, Late Wide Man, on horseback.

My father, His Hair is Tied, holding horse.

My grandmother, the one who stayed behind and married a local man.

My mother, Altsohaasbaa, at 15 or 16.

Pa, the man mother married to help her take care of her 3 girls.

My son, Brent, and our sole surviving uncle.

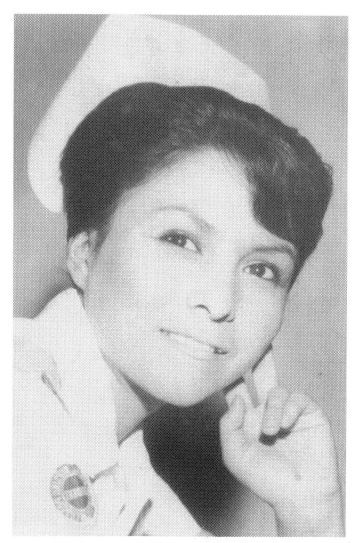

LPN training graduation in Dallas, Texas.

Peyote meeting teepee.

My husband with Navajo Mountain in background.

My award winning corn.

My older daughter, Ann, and her husband, Jacob.

My younger daughter, Tara, and her husband.

Stephanie, our All-American Runner.

Allison/Chubby's puberty ceremony.

My grandson, Ashkie, on his horse.

Amanda at a baseball game.

4 year old Stephan Dineh at a T-Ball game.

My brothers, Pa's boys.

My sisters and I, the keepers of the Naashgali Clan.

My husband's father, Jack To'aheedliinii, famous story teller.

Me and my sheep.

Climbing the Great Wall of China.